Life, University And Everything In Between:

the modern man's guide to uni life and not cocking it all up

K Daniel

Email: kdanielauthor@hotmail.com

ISBN:151972943X
ISBN-13: 9781519729439

DEDICATION

To Grasshopper and your ability to laugh with the world.

CONTENTS

ACKNOWLEDGMENTS

For ring-fencing my time and not making me do the washing up when I'm trying to focus I have my wife Andrea to thank. Also my thanks for Murphy and Boomer for generously and persistently bringing me varied bones, tennis balls and ropey thing whilst I'm trying to concentrate.

Chapter 1: On your marks, get set...

Your first day of university is likely to be one of your most self-induced stressful events to date. Okay, standing up in crown court to tell the magistrate that you're really sorry for overdosing the neighbour's yappy dog with laxatives is likely to be pretty anxiety provoking too, however for most of us day one at uni is also a bit of a buttock clencher. You may well feel that this is the moment you will officially fly the nest, albeit temporarily in many cases. Additionally your parents might be thinking this is the day that they can finally add some extra rental income with you finally out of the picture and have already booked the locksmith. Either way, you will be going away for a least a few months before you're likely to return home, and if you're 18, young, dumb and full of god knows what, then this is a quite possibly a really big and important step for you.

You might have a university in mind or are possibly already officially enrolled on some course. You may be the sort to have mapped out your career to the level of detail where you already know by what age your salary will hit £100,000 and in which costal town you plan on buying your second property. Or you might also be like many others, whose university choice consists of a "what uni will accept me with these grades" attitude and a healthy role of the dice to decide what you're going to study. Either way, if you don't feel at least some level of apprehension before you go, then you're either not a regular human or now is the time to step into that rehab programme. Whatever your background, please take solace in the fact that you are in the same wobbly boat as just about everyone else out there, but also take heart; the choice you've made to go to uni is likely to be one of the better ones you've made. You're about to step into a world that is both bigger and a lot more fun that you ever imagined.

Ask any member of the uni academic staff and they'll tell you that going to uni is all about working really hard and throwing yourself into your studies with more vigour and enthusiasm than a Viking raiding party on big hat day. That said, there is another side altogether. Most people don't simply turn up to study and then go home for the day. It's not the same as school and believe it or not, at university you are considered to be a proper adult. No-one's going to tell you to go stand outside the headmaster's office if you pratt around in class. You're allowed to smoke and drink. Also if you consistently act like a complete arse you'll simply be given an official letter that forcibly says "go away". You are going to be living amongst a bunch of people who, just like you, are going to be discovering what this uni thing is all about, bit by bit.

Uni is bigger than the studies and the staff. It's bigger than you and your expectations. It also has more depth, width and substance than what you can imagine at this point. It's also about the myriad of people who are going to be there with you and what experiences, character and baggage you all bring to the party. Therefore there is only so much prep work you can really do. Obsessing over which particular brand of pen will serve you best is not going to help you much at this stage. Anticipation of future events is only natural, but worrying about the specifics of what might happen at a place you've yet to go, with people you've yet to meet, is probably a bit exhausting. So take a break from yourself and if you can, try and take a lighter hearted approach to the whole business. Some of the pages of this book are written with a level of seriousness equivalent to penguins in wellies, however much of the underlying substance is hopefully meaningful, practical and is going to help you on your journey.

About this guide

There is a good guide to university. There is a good
guide to your freshers' year. In fact there is a multitude
of good guides to just about anything in this world: a
guide to fitness, a guide to dieting, a guide to Guiding,
and probably somewhere an A-Z illuminating the path
for those looking to find the best guides out there.
These precious manuscripts endeavour to enlighten the
way to those of us seeking a clearer route through life's
muddy waters, and in doing so highlight the *proper*
methods of how to go about things: how you quit
smoking, stop eating too much, manage your finances...

However, take a moment to think about the typically
sterile content of most of these manuscripts. Do most of
them portray real life? Or do they simply offer a
subjective one size fits all manual? At some point many
of us spontaneously take the time to go out to a
bookshop and seek answers to that which we truly
already know. Take dieting for example. Years ago I
read a book about losing weight and getting fit. I may
carry a few more extra pounds of tubby love than some
others, so in a moment of weakness I walk into the
bookshop and reach up for my copy of *Get Skinny,
Fatso* from a shelf which is placed just high enough to
expose my love handles. I take it home and in eager
anticipation read, from cover to cover, what I expect
will finally be the answer I was looking for: the key to

the secret knowledge of the fit and far sexier me. The revelation (and emotional deflation) I was so eager to find: stop shovelling it in porky and go buy some trainers.

The simple problem is those guides/instruction manuals/etc. are often not truly based in reality and frequently prey on our weaknesses when instead they should be trying bolster our strengths and motivation. They say "do this" when the message ought to read "consider this". Ladies sometimes look at fashion magazines for inspiration only to end up just feeling fat and deflated. That manual showing you how to build the Scandinavian flat pack wardrobe is helpful to a point, that is until three hours later when you are beginning to feel the need to stab someone in the eye because you have ten screws too few and an extra piece that looks important but won't give any clues to where it should have gone. What happens when you need to deviate from the guide because reality simply won't fit?

And this is where *this* guide comes in. It does not pretend to be superior to those other Muppet's guides in any way whatsoever. You will not learn anything revelationary about how you *must* think and behave when you attend university for the first time, so you should not read this as another concrete rules of do's and don'ts for the aspiring perfect student (this is also because these creatures are few and far between, and whilst there are some hard working, honest, law abiding, sober, socially functional and exceptionally moral young students out there, they already know how to budget, find the cleanest digs and work hard. They've also probably been doing their own washing and ironing since they were five and in most likelihood have a firm belief that beer is the urine of Satan and *sex* outside of the bedroom simply means "one more than five" (but only if you're speaking German)). So where this book does highlight some dos and don'ts, it's often done with a pinch of salt, and gives the reader some credit by assuming you have a greater IQ than the average jellyfish.

Neither is this one of the so called *survival manuals* to uni life. Believe it or not, whilst going to uni can be a bit anxiety provoking, you are not actually being air dropped behind enemy lines. No, this book is more of a tongue in cheek, warts 'n all, pit-falls manual for the average mucker looking to leave home for the first time, setting sail to sunny uni (yes, including Aberystwyth) and wanting to get an honest feel for what might be on the horizon. If you need to know how to effectively budget for the week on exactly £5.53 or bake a cake from freeze dried pasta and last week's dogs dinner, well there are books for all that. However, in the interests of a little bit of reality orientation for a moment, being able to take a look into someone else's real life university experiences, joys, laughs and tears might bring with it some valuable insight and a human perspective of the uni life you are undertaking. It can be a bit daunting, and quietly admitting it to yourself does not make you a lily livered, paranoid, apron string holding kindergartener. However the very fact that you're reading this means that you have some realistic concerns and are making positive moves to address them. The purpose of what you're reading is in many ways designed to promote confidence in your own ability to walk into the next few years with your head up and eyes open.

What, where and how?

By this point you may have already sorted out what you are going to study and where you plan to go and make your mark on the academic map, however if not, there are some considerations you might want to make. Firstly, you need to choose the subject of your study. You should hopefully have some vague idea of what you want to do in life and so know what to study, but herein lies the first hurdle where many trip up (as I did first time around). The problem is that many people start with the premise that they know what they want to do in respect to their career, because they have a firm idea in their head that they simply know, for example, that to be a doctor or lawyer is a good thing to be. Thus they go off to study law or medicine and consequently become terrible doctors or lawyers when they would possibly have made far better engineers or musicians.

Alternatively the flip side of the coin is to consider, first of all, what makes you really tick. Imagine the perfect dream career, and then take from this the best aspects of what makes those jobs exciting, interesting or worthwhile. If your dream job would be to be a rock star for example, the reasons for this might be because you like being creative, you like daily excitement and you enjoy influencing people. Therefore studying agriculture at uni for three years might be counterproductive when you could be studying journalism or drama and encompassing activities and aspects of what you love in your learning.

So picture what you see others doing that seems exciting (even if you realistically feel it's out of your reach) and take from it the best aspects that appeal, then apply that thought to what you might enjoy studying. When we enjoy an activity, we stand a far better chance at becoming really good at it. I have two degrees, the first of which was in Theology. Now whilst this was an interesting subject to study and I had a great time at uni (and no disrespect to the God Squad out there), if I were to walk into a church there is a good chance I might just be struck down by lightning. At the end of my three years I had made some good friends and could also change a beer barrel with my eyes closed, however on a practical note my degree led to very little at the time. It's really worth taking the time to have a proper reflection of what you really want to be doing with your life after you finish uni, *before* you actually start it. You plan your destination before you start a journey after all. Whilst this might seem more blatant than a brick in the teeth, you'd be surprised at the number of people signing off three years of their life with more consideration for what the uni bike shed looks like than what they will actually be studying. So decide before you go, that to the best of your knowledge, experience and imagination what you really think you want to do afterwards. Three or four years are a long time to be studying astrophysics to find out you really wanted to be a torturing small animals in veterinary school.

Once we have a firm and well thought out idea of what we are going to study, we then need to decide where we want to go. There is something to be said for drawing an imaginary 50 mile circle around where your parents live and making sure you don't apply anywhere inside. Think of it as a metaphorical nuclear fallout zone. The risk of ignoring this advice is the temptation to return home every five minutes when you've exhausted the pot noodle varieties or need your pants deloused. You are at uni, not simply to bury your head in the books, but to learn to live a little and stand on your own two feet. It's surprising, the number of young adults out there who are still swinging from the umbilical cord, can barely tie their own shoe laces, and for whom changing the fuse in the plug usually involves buying a new toaster. Therefore travelling beyond shouting distance from ma and pa and starting to think of your uni digs as home will serve you well in the long run. For some this will be a little uncomfortable at first; however what doesn't kill us...

Other considerations of the discerning applicant should involve the quality of the course. Go on the web and find out about the university's reputation. Are they simply after large student numbers to fill their courses and financial deficits or is it a sought after uni because of the excellent standards of teaching they deliver? Does the uni provide stats about the number of students going on to find jobs in their chosen field of study following graduation? What are the halls of residence and campus facilities like? Do the halls look clean and fresh or do they resemble a crime scene in a crack house? Is there a cash machine on campus or would you need to employ a Tibetan mountain guide with mule to find the nearest bank? Furthermore what's on offer outside of the campus? Is the uni putting too much emphasis on selling its location rather than what it has on offer on site?

Go and have a look. It might seem daft, but many people apply for a course without bothering to go and take a firsthand look at the place. Not all, but there are considerable numbers of students I've met who barely did the basics in respect to taking a simple reconnaissance mission to the local area. When I first went to uni I was lucky enough to have a friend who had gone to the same uni a year before me. However rather than simply take his word for what a fantastic place it was, I arranged to go and stay with him for a weekend. I got to crash in his halls, meet his friends, eat the canteen food on offer and get mashed in the local bar with other students. I met a few contacts from the rugby club and also met a few key players in the Ents (entertainments) team. I also earned a hangover made of the stuff of legends and when I returned to attend the university interview a few weeks later I was able to talk about how much I wanted their uni over all others and already knew how well I'd fit in. It soon felt that the interviewer was trying to sell the course to me rather than the other way around. Additionally when I showed up for freshers' week there were already some friendly faces I recognised, including the lad that remembered me for leaving an impression of my backside on the bonnet of his mother's car (but that's another story - and not in the way you might think!). If you have an opportunity to take a detailed look on the inside then take it. If not, well at least go for an exploratory open day visit.

Top tip: So you have your course and location in your sights. I've personally discovered the benefit, that in order to further your application, it never hurts to write a grovelling handwritten letter to the vice-chancellor (cc. the course leader) saying how much you desperately love their university and want to study there. At this point in your academic career this action might portray you as the sort of student that they want in their ranks and score you a few extra brownie points at interview.

Preparation

Whilst each individual will have an essential list of personal things they can't live without, getting some of the basics right might save you an extra trip back home because you remembered the 50 inch plasma but forgot to pack trousers. I mention this from personal experience, however there is no magic must have list. Think sensibly on this point. Having less than one pair of underpants is not going to win you any popularity points with the ladies, especially when you start to fester after a few days. Also brushing your teeth and the occasional dab of soap and water is important, so don't forget to take the basic hygiene essentials. On the flip side, it's highly unlikely there will be a need to cart along all of your old A-Level folders, unless of course you're likely to need kindling material to ward off a cold winter in your selected halls of residence.

Remember to pack a selection of clothing before you embark. If you're planning on joining a one-robe-fits-all religious cult you can skip this directive, otherwise a cross section of your wardrobe is going to be desirable. Also, you are in all likelihood going to be doing your own washing, so having something to wear other than your dressing gown when you do so is a big plus. A balanced approach here will save you carting loads off stuff with you at the expense of other essentials.

Other things you <u>don't</u> need to take include:

- The family pet.

- The wheelbarrow load full of condoms that you are optimistically hoping you'll need (there will be places that supply these where you are going). This includes the three industrial strength rubber, extra super double protection condoms your mum gave you "just in case" on your sixteenth birthday. (You could take them anyway however. They might have more in common with a chemical warfare or radiation suit, but it'll keep her happy and you never know when you might need a swimming cap). Also forget that nasty tired old rubber dunky that's been leaving its tell tale ring in your wallet for the last five years, unless of course the prospect of father-hood or a trip to the GUM clinic sounds like fun.

- House plants the size of coconut palms.

- Stereo systems big enough to require logistical support from Pickford's Travel.

- Family photo albums (you'll see them again, unless of course they see this as the golden opportunity to move whilst you're gone).

- More than one pair of sunglasses. You're cool enough.

- An emergency air drop Red Cross sized supply of food.

- Your porn/sex toy collection. Seriously. You don't want to be accidentally spied unloading an inflatable/rubber/leather anything on day one.

- Your mates. They'll still be in the pub talking about the same old crap when you return in the holidays.

- Your old nicknames. You no longer need to be called that which you were affectionately known as in the play ground since you were 13. "Tossface" or "Chunderbuckets" can safely be left at home. At uni you will earn a whole new plethora of affectionate put downs, so no need to add to the mix.

Other things you <u>might</u> need include:

- Passport photos. Whilst many universities these days are high tech enough to have cameras set up to take an instant photo of you, if not you'll have to go sit in a photo booth and will have a permanent "I hate queues, I'm so bored" look on your face on your various ID's for the next three years.

- Your basic documentation the uni sent you. This will include stuff like a map of campus and the local area, bus routes, useful phone numbers, your course timetable, etc. You're going to look a bit of a sad puppy wandering around the place looking for your room when everyone else is getting settled into the fun and frolics going on in the uni bar.

- Soap or equivalent. Absolute minimum hygiene requirement Stinky Pants.

- Money and ready access to your prearranged bank overdraft. If you're going to have to sell your soul to get through uni financially, you might as well do what you can in advance. You will likely need it soon enough anyway.

All that said, take consideration to how much you can carry, unless of course you're lucky enough to have the butler deliver you and everything you can't bear to live without. Also take in to account that you're unlikely to be moving in to the penthouse suite of the Ritz. Uni halls tend to be modelled on minimal requirement self storage containers if you're lucky, or chicken coops if you're not. I remember my old bed in my first halls of residence; you were at serious risk of unexpectedly and rapidly meeting the floor boards if you turned over too quickly. Furthermore, if you opened the wardrobe you would hear everything going on in the room next door (as it was partly built into their room).

Once you arrive be prepared to queue like you've never queued before. Be prepared to be more patient than a hypochondriac at a pathological diseases convention. However once you're done, (so long as you remembered all of your documentation) you're done. Then it's home sailing and time to get to know some of the most interesting, fun, odd and possibly best friends you will ever have. You're about to commence with freshers' week and whilst you will definitely remember the start of it you might be hard pushed to recall the end.

One final introductory note: I have written this book from a predominantly (although not exclusively) male perspective. The reason for this is hopefully obvious. I have purposefully not tried to disguise this on the basis that writing a manual about three years of someone's life, based on my own experiences, is after all pretty subjective. All of the content, even that which is slightly tongue in cheek, has a grounding in my own memories of one of the best times of my life. Thus to try and make this overly generic would be to omit an honest component that lends itself towards the humorous tones in which it is meant to be read. That being said, the accessibility this book is not designed to be exclusively dependent on whether you have a tinky or a winky. Where I mention "mates" imagine I wrote "bezzies" and the advice is still solid. The life lessons in further chapters contain much what is relevant to all students whether you're sporting a whole bush worth of testosterone fuelled chest hair or have ovaries the size of watermelons. Quite simply this is not just for boys, but it is unashamedly angled from that perspective in parts.

Chapter 2: Freshers' week

Freshers' week is the initial and vital commencement of uni life everywhere. It will be your starting block to the next three years and is also where you will get to meet all the other noobs (who are just as scared and in the same leaky boat as you). At some universities freshers' week starts a week earlier than most of the other second and third year students returning, so as to allow you time to get settled in and leave your own scars on the uni bar without the big kids feeling the need to prove they rule the roost.

> *Top tip: It's also when you will have a golden opportunity to set the benchmark by which all other students will be judged (so your fellow students will still be telling tales years*

later of how cool, suave, sophisticated and cultured you are). It might also be the platform from which you accidentally re-launch your career as Chunderbuckets. So be careful, and if you overdo it, just don't overdo it more than the other guy.

The freshers' week timetable

There will be a plan for freshers' week. It's by no accident that first years travel about the local town from pub to pub, consuming all in sight like an plague of locusts. Freshers' week is typically arranged by a veteran student team with the specific goal of getting everyone to settle in to uni life from the very start. This needs a degree of organisation, planning, adaptability and a highly developed sense of humour. That's where the Ents team (entertainments team or equivalent) come in. They're the sort of students that whilst they want to have an involvement in the student union, and do give a genuine monkey's about their fellow student's welfare, they're also probably a little on the, let's say, bouncy personality side. Make prolonged eye contact at your own peril. You'd know the Ents team by the fact that if the world was ending in five minutes time, they'd be the ones in the middle of the dance floor still doing the Macarena.

The timetable will most likely start with some sort of introduction meeting. This is worth attending purely on the basis of recognising who is going to be planning your miniature invasion of the local and once respectable establishments. At three in the morning, the ability to recognise one of those faces might just be your ticket to a taxi home, along with someone who has a vague idea as to where they're going. Also, by attending the meet, you'll get an idea of all the exciting things in store for you and your new found friends. Thus, when there are limited tickets for the coach load off to somewhere exciting, it will be other people's sorry backsides left in an uneventful uni bar. Get a copy of what's going on and stick it up somewhere in your room.

One of the main features of the week, as I vaguely recall, is the obligatory pub crawl. Sounds simple enough? And it even starts in a reasonably uniform fashion. I remember we were split up into groups of 10 or so and were guided around the local pubs and bars in a vaguely pre-planned order. The rules were one drink in each establishment and simply try to make it to the end. Each team was given their own Ents rep, a starting pub and a route map. After a few hours it all became rather messy. We bumped into numerous other groups, lost members, found some others, met some very interesting dancers, ate questionable take away food, and all in all had a brilliant time. What was best of all though was the knowledge that we all had an exclusive story to tell from a night out that we alone shared with our group... our new friends. For my own experience and unknown to me to at the time, was that this was the night when I first met my future wife to be. However it's not all bad.

Getting to know people

When meeting other students for the first time you will likely start with asking and being asked questions around three subjects: your name, where you're from and what you're studying. You will possibly feel a little judged and will also most likely be trying to absorb all this new information about those you meet. Don't. Just remembering someone's name is good enough for a start and the other stuff can wait until later. People initially bumble around each other asking mundane questions because they feel socially awkward, however quickly try and move forward. Taking an interest in something more substantial than what someone is studying will make a better impression and is really not that hard to do. Simply paying people compliments about their appearance or interests is a much better way forward. People like to talk about themselves and they'll in turn be more relaxed and interested in you if you show a genuine interest in them. So find something to talk about other than yourself and you'll be on to a winner to getting to know others in no time at all.

So when meeting new people, try and listen to them more, rather than double-barrelling them directly in the face with your opinions of all that's wrong with the world; they'll find you better company. Don't say every sentence that comes to mind and don't try too hard to impress. Note that whilst people tend to like individuals who are humorous, sarcasm will always sound far funnier in your head than it does in reality.

Good things to talk about:

- Their interest in sports.

- Their interest in music.

- Positive comments about their clothing and appearance.

- Why they like the uni you all came to.

- Other interesting people they have already met.

- Cool stuff going on in freshers' week.

Good things to say:

- "I like your jacket/shirt/shoes/etc."

- "This is a great uni to choose because..."

- "Need a refill?"

Not so good things to talk about:

- Your A–Level results.

- Why your area of study is intellectually superior to theirs.

- Why this is the last uni that would take you.

- Your previous sexual conquests.

- Your Pokemon collection.

- The three 1950's collector's edition condoms your mum gave you.

- General bullshit about you being formerly trained as a ninja, SAS operative or test pilot.

Not so good things to say:

- "Your round first."

- "Your roommate really lucked out"

- "Bucket please!"

- "Pull my finger."

It might also be worth considering getting to know other students who would otherwise normally be outside of your typical social circle back home. Introducing yourself to some of the international students can be a big plus and you may find yourself with friends all over the world by the end of your course. That might also put you in good stead for some post uni travelling too. Additionally, getting to know some of the mature students can also be a bonus. I remember meeting a guy starting uni in his 30's. He turned out to be one of the most well liked students on campus, the future president of the student union and also the drummer in our band. So spread your social wings and do not, whatever you do, prejudge others. This is hard, but try and recognise your own prejudices. Everyone has them, especially those that think they don't. And forgive those that struggle to talk about more than their A-Level results.

There is always a flip side to the coin, and in this instance there are some who might be better avoided, or at least taken with a pinch of salt. First on the list is any student whose main challenge in life is chuffing enough cannabis before breakfast in an attempt get higher than a weather balloon. We all know that there will be a mix at uni, from those who are all-out pot heads, to students who are not interested in any form of illicit substance, and others that are tempted to dabble a little. My suggestion is to avoid those who would desperately try to make being permanently away with the fairies a raison d'être. Also bloodshot eyes and perpetual conversation about where the next packet of biscuits is coming from is not generally considered attractive. More about illicit substances later, however drugs don't get into people's bloodstreams by themselves. There is always some Muppet peddling it hoping to find company with an equivalent IQ. Additionally the uni may just decide to crucify the first person they catch to the vice chancellors door in a bid to make an example.

Possibly another type for the avoid list are the tutors that frequent the student bar. This is not to say you can't socialise with those that teach however there are some that can be inappropriate at times, especially in the context of alcohol. Whilst some of the staff will no doubt be quite charismatic and charming people to know, others will be social misfits who struggle to get along with their own peers, hence find the student population so appealing. And nothing will stroke their ego better than a bunch of students who are keen to impress those that mark their work. I knew someone who became romantically involved with a lecturer for some time. Whilst they tried to keep this a secret, half of the students suspected there was more than some extracurricular tutoring going on and I wouldn't be surprised if the other staff had an idea too. So the advice here is don't get overly involved with the staff, especially those that appear a bit too keen.

Next on the list are the second year predators. That is not to say they're all a bunch of velociraptors however there are a minority of students who have managed to make it all the way through the first year and are now feeling like the big kids on campus. They've renamed it "fuck-a-fresher week" and it's now a big game of who can impress the most. These creatures are easily spotted though. Their natural habitat tends to be in and around the campus bar. They are also a pack animal and will often hunt as such. Stealth and subtlety is not in their vocabulary and so they're easy to spot, however their strength lies in their ability to make the innocent fresher target feel like they are somehow more of a proper grown up by socialising with them (the more experienced and superior second year). Their weapons of choice: the drinking game and cheap booze. They are also more likely to be blokes than women, but this is not exclusive, and the word of warning here is that whoever slips in the sack with one is likely to earn a reputation that will stick for some time. Keeping it a secret is not part of the game.

For some, one of the immediate dangers of being let off the parental leash is the tendency to mistakenly think that you're now officially a wise old owl, are socially mature and thus will only ever make insightful and informed choices. Then when the rozzers pick you up at three in the morning for running around town, making a racket and sporting the latest in traffic cone headwear, you may feel your self esteem has taken a kick in the plums. University is partly about growing up; it's not an entry requirement. So last on the list of must-avoid people is anyone associated with the law. The police won't approach you to compliment you on your gentlemanly etiquette towards the staff in the local pub, but they will knobble you for exposing your bare backside to the passing traffic on the spur road. So the lesson here is simple: if what you're thinking of doing is likely to attract the special attentions of the local boys in blue, don't do it.

Social media

In modern times, thanks to the wonders of social media, we are all able to connect and interact with each other in a way that mankind has never comprehended historically. Computers, phones, tablets and other devices allow us to know who's dating who, who's been where, who likes what and who is really skiving when they should be in lectures. This can be wonderful when getting to know each other and finding shared interests that might not otherwise be so obvious.

A word of warning here: by all means allow social media to supplement your life, but not the other way around. I find it ironic how some people go out for the evening and appear more interested in messaging people who are not there rather than speaking to the ones who actually are. Additionally your friends may well be interested in that one great photo of you getting arrested for indecent exposure however please don't kid yourself that anyone is in any way interested in piccies of your dinner and every drink you have. Those that have to advertise, and in real time, to all and sundry about what a great time they're having are more than likely kidding themselves. When you're having the time of your life, chances are you won't have opportunity to be running a minute by minute newsflash update that is paralleled only by the media coverage at the start of the Gulf War.

Who you connect to electronically is worth consideration also. Your new chums may well find those images of you sleeping in your own puke hilarious, but Auntie Ethel on the other hand may have a sense of humour failure. So bear a thought to being disinherited when you consider who you allow access to your digital life online. Additionally there is some chance that you might want to be employed in the future. Documentary evidence about what a plonker you can be at times might not sit well when you're trying to convince your potential employer about what an upstanding model citizen you are. Employers are known to take a peek into social media sites for this very reason. This might seem a million miles away at this point however electronic photos don't fade. Thought should also be given to socially connecting with tutors on line (even the cool ones). There may come a time when you're desperately trying to convince one of the lecturers to give you an essay extension because you're dying of some tropical disease. This might not wash when they just caught the latest uploaded image of you chugging a beer whilst sporting the latest in toga fashion. As the saying goes: behind every successful student is a deactivated Facebook account.

Freshers' week is fun. Record some of it for posterity. Social media connections will possibly be important to your start at uni and there will be a lot of good stuff on there; just don't get bogged down in virtual living when real life is so much more fun.

Freshers' fair

One of the main events of freshers' week is the fair. You will be invited to attend this event so make a special note to self to make sure that you do. Freshers' fair is where you will have an opportunity to find out all about the various clubs and societies that are going on in and around uni. This is also the event where you can sign up to everything from the debating team and fine art appreciation society to the yard of ale club or finding out in which cellar to hide with dungeon master and all the other RPG anoraks. There will be something for everyone and this is a golden opportunity to get involved in events or activities that will allow you to meet others with similar interests.

Many people tend to sign up for more than they can chew and there is no problem with this. You might only ever turn up to one event of *Trainspotting,* realise it's nothing to do with cult films, and never again darken their platforms and clipboards. This doesn't matter. What does though is missing the fair and not finding out what's out there.

This is also your opportunity to discover what's happening with all the sporting aspects of your uni. Get involved from day one and you won't feel like a Billy-no-mates joining the football or rugby team half way through the term. Also no one wants to do a rugby team initiation ceremony on their own (trust me) so get signed up at the first opportunity, or risk doing *the dance of the flaming arseholes* as a solo performance.

There might also be companies or associations

attending the fair. If you happen to be doing a vocational degree this could be where you first get to link in with people you might end up working for. It might provide a bit of focus early on and let's not forget the most important thing: all the freebies they want to hand out. Students love freebies more than fishmonger's wives appreciate deodorant.

The end of the beginning

When all's said and done, after your first week at uni, there will be certain expectations laid on you. Freshers' week is designed to get all the new students settled in and to plug the homesick blues. It's also supposed to be a bit of a wild and fun introduction to campus life and will attempt to provoke you to come out of your shell a little. If you feel that this is only the tip of the iceberg to three years of getting completely mullered then you might want to reconsider why you're going to uni in the first place. There will of course be plenty of social events throughout the next three years, such as the summer ball, rag week and other such excuses to go wild, but as with anything in life, a healthy balance of things is frequently the more sensible option.

A few more points about freshers' week: Take the time

to explore. Not just campus but go out into the city/town/countryside/mountains. Find the best coffee shops and check out the menus at the local places to eat. Get your timetable sorted. Make sure you've settled in to your digs and at least unpack some of your stuff. Know your way to the lecture halls and get signed on to everything you need to, i.e. library passes, uni computer sign on, canteen vouchers, beg from your bank manager, whatever. The point being that if you get these things done at the start, it's much less of a pain in the backside in the long run. When you need to get that particular library book out that has a limited number of copies, you'll be grateful when you can stroll right in, whilst others are stuck in the sign up queue that looks more like the complaints line for VW owners outside of a Beastie Boys concert.

Turn up on time. First impressions really do count. If you irritate the person that's going to be marking your work on day one by showing up an hour late, smelling of margaritas and wearing mismatched shoes, then don't be surprised when they get picky with your essays. Also take the time to be polite to your lecturers. They work hard for not the greatest salary in the world and might appreciate the odd "thank you" at the end of a seminar or lecture. Also lecture halls are not opportunities to catch up on much needed sleep. I recall a particular Monday morning lecture that always had a comedy moment at around 09:20, when one of my fellow students, guaranteed and without fail, would be snoring with enough force to register on the Richter scale. He didn't make it to the second year. So be nice to the staff and treat them as you would want to be treated in their stead.

The Student Union

At each uni there will be a Student Union (SU) with the purpose of directing student events and also representing you and your fellow colleagues to the university faculty. There will be an elected president of the SU who will oversee what's going on. They are elected democratically, as is the vice president and several other positions within the SU. They are typically students that have some experience in uni life and are genuinely interested in providing help and support to all students at the uni. They work hard for almost nothing other than the simple gratitude of you and your colleagues, so be polite. Take the time to get to know who they are and if they ask for student support in setting up an event or club, why not get involved? Pay heed to SU notices and don't forget to actively vote when you are given the opportunity. And when you have been at uni for a reasonable period of time and start to feel a bit more savvy, maybe you might want to put yourself up for election for one of the positions. It won't do your future CV any harm and you might just have a bit of a scream in the process.

A final word

Freshers' week is all about you and the other noobs, so make every effort to get stuck in there and enjoy it to the full. Sign up for stuff, make loads of new friends and go to as many of the organised events as you can. And whilst making the most of it, try and recall that uni life is going to be bigger and wider than this first week alone, so don't burn yourself out completely. Also try and apply a little more organisational skill than simply remembering to change your pants and getting mashed, and the mark you make in the first week might just pay off over the next three years.

> *Top tip: In your first few weeks on campus find your very own fortress of solitude. There is a toilet somewhere on campus that very few people know the location of and because of this it'll always be pristine clean and smelling of roses.*

Chapter 3: Academia

You're here to study. Well... that's not entirely true is it? It would be more accurate to say that *one* of the main reasons you are here is to study. You're also here to learn about life, to grow a little and to have a crack at letting go of the apron strings. If university was solely about studying it would be far cheaper and more straight forward to just do it over the internet. And this is what some choose to do if it suits their lifestyle, however for most, the combined experience is the one of value. Still, whilst the living experience is an essential element in this whole business, if it's all play and no work, then your university venture is likely to last about as long as an overly confident fox at a beagle convention. So be prepared to put in some graft, and let's not forget that this is the area of study that *you* chose to immerse yourself in. So try and enjoy it. Sometimes studying may get a little dry or dull, however the best way to combat this is to try and actively lose yourself in it. Take some pride in what you're doing, learn to love it, and hopefully your work will not only be your interest, but will become your passion. These are the people that succeed in this world.

The reading list

At the start of each of your differing modules you will be given a reading list. This is a list of books and journal articles that your module tutor will feel it important for you to get your head around. That's not to say they expect you to be able to read every last word of each of these references, but they do on the other hand hope you'll do more than use it as emergency toilet roll when the house funds run dry. They will want you to get your head around a couple of the major texts and at least have a flick through a few of the main chapters in the others.

It may also pay dividends to get yourself down to the library sooner than later, before all of the main texts go walkies and you're left with some dog-eared copy of a book that was published at a time when modern thinking meant you could almost sail around the world without falling off. Some students have a nasty tendency to hoard. There will be those on your course who will make a beeline for the library as soon as they have the reading list and take out every major text they can in a bid to minimise their own anxiety. They will then carry this half ton of books back to their digs and put them where they will not see sunlight for the next month or so until the essay is due. At his time they will read about a page and a half from each text in order to get their quote and reference for the half baked essay they are going to submit. This can't be helped and these people don't do this on purpose, but it is annoying and does happen frequently, so make sure you get down to the library early. Oh, and make sure you read the texts well before the date when your library fines start building up and they send in the bailiffs.

The academic timetable

In addition to the various reading lists you receive, you will also be presented with a course time table. This is a schedule of the various lectures and seminars you'll be required to attend. You don't have to be a skilled cryptographer or astrologer to divine any meaning from this but it may well help. It will most likely involve lots of times, numbers and letters that mean something to someone somewhere, however this is a closely guarded secret and the key to the translation lies in listening to your tutor explaining what it all means. Furthermore on the way to your very first lecture, don't stray from the beaten path and make sure you stay with the core group of your fellow students trying to figure out where the hell room B423c is, and whether the module is actually going on this term or next. That way, when you get lost and are inevitably late, you will all be late together. There is safety in numbers.

The other thing of note with the timetable is that this is not school anymore. They won't try and mollycoddle you to make sure you actually do turn up. It's now your responsibility to get up, find your cleanest skids and get yourself out of the door on time. Never again will you hear the word "detention" when you cock up; at uni they give you written notice to push off elsewhere (and a bill).

There will also be certain expectations laid on you. Initially these may be from your parents. They will in most likelihood be both proud of you and at the same time wishing you would only be just a little more mature in your attitude before letting you off the leash. They do want you to succeed. Your success reflects on them and their superior parenting skills, plus all they have invested in you for the last 18 or so years. Fail and they'll accept the excuses, but dad will always treat you like a bit of a thickie and mum will forever be saying "bless" after your name when she's talking to the neighbours.

Infinitely more important though are your own expectations. You chose to do this course (if not and someone else did this for you, well then, good luck). And in your acceptance of a place of study you have a chance to prove to yourself that you are capable of focus, determination and a bit of bloody hard graft at times. As already said above, be proud of what you achieve and prove your potential. When you succeed, try and do a little better. When you perform better, try and exceed. But when you fail, listen, learn and pick yourself up with more vigour than a rabbit in a Viagra factory.

Learning

One of the newest teaching methods available to universities these days is online learning. There is a tendency for some departments to be highly reliant on this as it does, after all, offer value for money. E-learning will mean that you can go over the teaching material as much as you need. You also don't have to put your hand up to stop the flow of the lecture. Additionally you can avoid those uncomfortable moments of being caught by the tutor, whose seminar you just skipped, when you're seen an hour later in the campus bar.

The down side however is that some people really struggle to engage with computers. Furthermore, some e-learning packages record what you've looked at and some offer mandatory questions at the end to check you have not only read but understood the material. This might seem like a good idea at first, but when university becomes so prescriptive, it sometimes subdues individual effort. This type of learning can easily remove personal reward for good work in place of punishment for laziness or complacency. Queen Victoria's Great Britain would be pleased.

A quick mention here about note taking. Your lecture notes are to provoke memories of what you have been taught. Unless you're training as a court stenographer you will struggle to get everything down. Lectures are supposed to spur your reading and thought processes as you study in your own time outside of lectures. Uni is not about being spoon fed the answers, and simply turning up to lectures with more pens than WH Smiths won't help you learn. Think of the lecture as the trailer to the main feature. So don't get hell bent on recording more irrelevant detail than the local train-spotting club. Additionally students that take laptops in to lectures are in for a hard time. It might make them feel like they're able to take comprehensive notes and have access to the course material and internet all at the same time, but the unfortunate reality is that this is likely to lead to info overload. Use a pen and paper to serve as little reminders to what you are actively listening to, then study afterwards in your personal time. Remember this is not school and the uni will expect you to be wearing big pants by now, so go do three or four hours personal study in the library for every one hour of lecture time. Even the thickies can't fail with this simple resolve.

Mobile phones; what bigger distraction can you have? Turn them off for your own sake. Your lecturer will get mega pissed at you if it goes off audibly or you are seen checking out your number of Facebook likes of that pic of you accidentally vomiting over your roommate's toothbrush. Also, texting your mates in the same room as you, and in front of your tutor, is far more obvious than you might think, so don't do it. Furthermore if you can vary the place where you generally sit in class you might find that this helps with retaining good concentration. Whilst it is nice and comforting to sit next to your friends all the time, if you can avoid always sitting at the back of the class you might be doing yourself a really big favour. Another good turn you can do yourself is to try and sit next to those who tend to be interested in actually doing the work. Enthusiasm is contagious, as is pissing about. If you occasionally place yourself next to others who are keen, then you're more likely to pay attention and actually learn something. Sitting next to the class comedian might be entertaining, however the campus bar might be the better place to associate with the local buffoon.

Essays, procrastination and the last minute wonder

After you've attended a bunch of lectures and seminars there will be an essay due. Note that they will more than likely set the essay question well before your module began, and the crazy idea with this is that you start work on it before you actually complete the series of lectures. They may also have some far out notion that you will have been reading all those books you took out from the library which are in actual fact now performing a useful service as your draught excluder. The pit fall here is procrastination. If you don't know what this means then look it up later, sometime, maybe. Unfortunately good intentions don't write good essays. The trick is to not overwhelm yourself in the mountain of work you have to manage. It might work in your favour to start with breaking it down into more digestible chunks. Set yourself mini goals or targets of reading chapters and then take notes. If you can manage this:

- You will feel like you are starting to succeed.

- You might actually be learning and understanding some of what they are talking about in lectures.

- You will have the bulk of your essay mostly

written in note format before you even start.

Preparation of your study area is also important. You might find, like many, that the library is your place of choice due to the whole study-serious atmosphere in there and the lack of distraction from your housemates playing bog roll football. A quiet and regular corner of the library might just help you manage a good and healthy work/play routine. Alternatively, some like to know they have their home comforts at hand and don't want the hassle of bike chaining their laptop to the radiator every time they need a wizz. Either way, make sure your work area is relatively clear of clutter. It's amazing how easily distracted we can be when our subconscious is telling us to rest when we really need to get that piece of work done. Don't have the TV on! You'll even be drawn into cbeebies if it's there. When it's time for your essay to be handed in, if you honestly know more about the adventures of Dipsy and Tinky Winky than you do about your chosen subject, you won't be making your folk back home proud. Furthermore, there is no need to go overboard in the other direction. There's no call for wearing blinkers, locking your roommate out and laminating all of your lecture notes. A clean and tidy study area, with and a little space to spread, is all that's generally needed.

The alternative to having neglected your studies is the last minute wonder. This is the all-nighter special essay that is mysteriously formulated in the final 12 hours before the due time. It will somehow magically come together in a caffeine induced, waking coma state of mind in the early hours. You will most likely have a miniature pre-midlife crisis moment at minus 12 hours, followed by the revelation that you have some old lecture notes that are semi-readable, and you sort of got the gist of some of the stuff they were talking about in a seminar. You'll also remember that dog eared copy of a book you managed to get out last week and despite Ye Olde English it's written in, you'll start reading like you never have before. The real tragedy with this scenario is the sad revelation that, as you're hashing together your elastoplast essay, you might actually begin to have an understanding and genuine interest in what you're doing. And when you get your scrape through result you'll know that you were capable of so much more.

Top tip: There is one, eleventh hour save for an essay that is due, when you haven't got your act together in time to get it done. The extension request. *Use this with extreme caution. Remember these people you're trying to blag are highly trained academics. Whilst some may have little by way of common sense and for many, boiling an egg is considered the height of self*

> **sufficiency, they are not stupid. They**
> **will figure out pretty soon that you**
> **should only have a limited supply of**
> **deceased grannies.**

Putting it all together

Writing the essay has to take into account several factors and the first and most important of these is the essay question itself. This may seem a little obvious, however missing the point before you've even started is a bit like setting sail on the party yacht before realising you got on the wrong boat and have in fact gate-crashed an exclusive wedding party (ref. my Uncle Dave et al ☺ circa 2004). It's too late by the time you've handed it in to do anything about it, so please read the question. Break it down into its respective parts and understand what it's asking. Don't get carried away and start writing irrelevant crap simply because your motivation and creativity joined forces and found a better outlet than playing with Lego.

The next obvious but common cock up is the word count. Historically, the solution to not failing the word count trap was to simply write with bigger handwriting and not use both sides of the paper. And let's face it, it takes one lonely, sad and neurotic essay marker to sit there and count your word total. Unless they really hate you of course and want to teach you a lesson for always turning up to their lectures three hours late. However, in modern times this job is taken care of by the word processor, so you need to be careful, as for some reason lecturers are very precious about you producing either too much or (more likely) too little. The argument goes that in order to answer any given question, the perfect response to this should always be done in blocks of typically either 2,500 or 5,000 words. More than 10% either way and ye gods will smite thee. Answer your essay with an internationally published literary prize winner of a paper at 2,249 words and you may as well run for the hills Ma Parker. Incidentally I know a student who was officially criticised for producing a piece of work that was exactly 2,500 words on the dot for being a smart arse.

In respect to the form and content of your written masterpiece, it's not rocket science (unless of course you are actually studying missile propulsion). You start with an introduction. Think of this as a chat up line. It's a quirky little bit at the start to catch the reader's attention and lets them know your general intentions. It's not the core of the essay, so don't give away any of the good stuff, just hint at it. The middle bit is, well... the middle. You've either studied and researched all you can, in which case this bit will almost write itself, or if not, this is where the wafflers and blaggers get to practice their art. Then there is the conclusion. Think of this as the "thanks for that darlin', now shut the door on your way out" bit.

Write for your audience. You will most likely know the person who is going to mark your work. You may like them and they may like you. Alternatively they may hate your guts and you might feel they are the devil incarnate, but still, they are the one that will judge your work. If you produce a personal attack that completely shreds their core beliefs and their speciality, then expect criticism. Whilst at risk of sounding like this is a suggestion to butt-kiss, please don't misunderstand. If you disagree with some of what they taught then have a watertight, well researched and referenced argument that is diplomatically put forward in an intellectual manner. They want to see insight, not cockiness. They are also not expecting you to present them with a piece of work that will send their spell checker into a seizure. Proof read it before you hand it in.

Pitfalls with essays are easy to come by and none more so than the referencing list or bibliography. The problem here is not in documenting which book, journals or websites that you have obtained your information from. The issue that many a pedantic marker will have is the referencing system that the uni deems to be acceptable. Many use the Harvard

Referencing system however there are variations. This is essentially the format in which the references should be laid out at the end of your work. It's not enough to get the author, date of publication, title, edition and publisher listed in alphabetical order and in a certain font and size, it also needs to be feng shui approved and written on a night when the planets are aligned in Capricorn. You *will* lose marks here at some point. Try and get most of it right.

Most courses will also require you to produce a dissertation towards the end of your study. You will have until your third or final year to ruin your underwear on this one, however it will come about quicker than a bishop in a brothel. The dissertation is essentially the biggest single piece of work you are likely to produce at uni. It's basically an essay that will be somewhere in the region of 10,000-15,000 words long (plus or minus 10%, not 10.5!). You will be expected to produce a reference list of biblical proportions and actually to have read some of them too. Be warned, this one doesn't work well with the "I work best under pressure" attitude or as a last minute wonder. You will be given what feels like a decade to get started on this. My advice is to start some serious research yesterday, then try and catch up.

***Top tip: Turning off your internet
connection on your computer and***

mobile phone as you write your essay will help you. It's a little difficult to concentrate on what you're doing with your friends bombarding you with texts about what time the party is starting and you receiving mildly threatening emails from your mum asking if you remembered Great Aunt Gertrude's birthday.

Exams

One of the most anxiety provoking times at uni will be when it's exam season. You will hear some interesting comments floating around the common rooms at this time of the year such as, "I'm no good at exams", "I don't write quickly enough", or "I don't respond well to the pressure". All these and more generally translate into "I haven't studied/attended lectures/know anything". No one really likes exams except those who really know their stuff. If you truly understand what you've been studying then these will be a breeze. Last minute cramming might get you a save if you're lucky.

Exam revision is best done in easily digestible chunks and started in plenty of time before the actual event.

Revision that commences whilst sat on the lav 20 minutes before the exam is due to start is about as much use as tits on a snake. Give yourself a run up. Also don't pull a caffeine fuelled all-nighter revision session before the exam date. If you can break your revision up into brief sessions each day, this will serve you well.

> *Top tip: Exam season can bring out the autistic spectrum side of us. If you find yourself not only writing a revision timetable, but are reaching for the coloured highlighters and laminator, then it's time to get some air.*

On the big day itself, even if you have studied, there are still some precautions you will have to take. The main one of these (besides turning up at the right, place, time, etc.) is avoiding the saboteurs. These are the students that float around the entrance of the exam hall seeking to ambush any semi-confident looking student with their woeful tales of harsh markers, broken pencils and difficult exam questions designed to trip you up. They will use any negative tactic, not to be horrible to you, but in a semi-conscious move to transfer some of their own anxiety because they spent all last week in the pub and the last 20 minutes in the toilet crying. Keep your head down and don't make eye contact, but you will see them floating and waiting to pounce.

Some people are just prone to mild panic attacks or heightened levels of anxiety at these times. Whilst these are most common with those who haven't done the work, it also serves to have a few tricks up your sleeve to minimise any of this. Some will tell you (usually in a rather panicky way), "remember to breathe". However, if you were prone to forgetting to do this, you would not likely have made it thus far. By far a better trick is to simply make a conscious effort to distract yourself, i.e. go sit somewhere comfortable and take a few quiet minutes to watch some TV, check your emails or get a coffee. Your knowledge is not going to abandon you if you stop thinking about all you have learnt this term for a moments R&R. Another trick to help you relax is to listen to a favourite album on your headphones before the start. That way other people are also less likely to try and clog your mind with their worries.

Once in the exam, a few pointers:

- Read the question.

- Make a few scratch notes as to how you are going to formulate your answer (do not write an essay on the side).

- Re-read the question.

- Write semi-legibly at least. There's no point in producing 10 sides of pure genius in hieroglyphs. It's far better to write slightly slower and be understood by the marker.

- Avoid waffle. 'Nuf said.

- Re-read the bloody question again and make sure you have understood what it's asking!

Presentations

Ask a room of students if they enjoy doing presentations and you'll be hard pushed to find many hands being raised (with possibly the exception of someone suffering a burst of clinical mania). People in general don't like standing up in front of others to be judged. That's what you go to court for. It's just not nice. They will make you do it however, because in real life, beyond the campus bar you will be faced with situations, when in your line of work you have to speak to other people and share information effectively. If you can stand up in front of your peers, without dribbling too much, and share a few thoughts in a way that doesn't involve the need to compassionately put you out of your misery, then bonus. The core truth of doing presentations is that the more you do, the better you will get at them. The trick is learning to do your first one without the need for incontinence pants.

Preparation is essential. If your material is well researched and you know your stuff then you give yourself a bit of contingency. You may well cock up half way through when you realise you left some of your notes in the stall, but you will be able to fall back on your actual knowledge rather than leaning on the rehearsed pantomime presentation you started with. You will have the ability to be adaptable and stand the danger of seriously sounding like you know what you're talking about. The main advantage though is that preparation will ground and minimise any jitters you may get.

How you deliver your presentation is also essential. Many people use PowerPoint. This is a superb tool for presentations but with it you run the risk of a commonly know side effect called *death by Power Point*. This is when your audience start enthused, bright eyed and bushy tailed, however within five minutes of you reading verbatim from the slides, you will have induced a trance like state that can be measured clinically on the Glasgow Coma Scale. Therefore if you can make your presentation a little different from the norm, not lean on your slides so heavily and use more than one tone of voice, you might also be reducing the rates of suicidal ideation and deliberate self harm amongst your peers.

Keeping your calm when you are up there is a matter of practice, not only with each presentation you do, but by having a few rehearsals beforehand. However, the trick with rehearsals is not simply in going through your material; you also need to practice how to keep your nerve. Some simple tricks:

- Regular and deep breathing. Smile and don't talk too quickly. Believe it or not, a mildly artificial smile has a positive psychological impact on your outlook. You'll also appear more confident. Don't overdo it however by looking like the models from the latest Aardman production.

- Look just slightly over the heads of the audience. Not making direct eye contact avoids the danger of your subconscious trying to read the facial expressions of your audience, hence distracting you from your thoughts. It'll still appear as if you're addressing them directly. Think of them as a gathering of angry nuns: address them collectively, politely and with respect, but make prolonged eye contact and they'll see right through your shenanigans.

- Having something to hold in your hands (pen, pointer, reference cards, etc.) will help reduce any obvious signs of anxiety such as hand wringing. But grip it, don't play with it. You'll look a complete numpty when you shatter your pen and the spring fires out at the audience.

- Don't dress ready for an arctic expedition. When nervous, your body temperature may rise a little, and if your armpits start getting slushy you may find yourself feeling self conscious.

- Don't carry a half ton of notes. Save a tree. As well as being more ecologically sound you don't stand the risk of reading word for word from your script. A few reminder cards are all you need. Get a highlighter pen and colour code certain key words for easy reference, so that when you look away you can easily find your place again.

- Dress smart and comfortable. It'll help you feel more professional. Also if you look the part, people are more likely to take notice of what you have to say. Dress like a chav and expect people to be watching their wallets more than your presentation.

- Go to the toilet before you start. Really. Just try.

- Beware the grammar Nazis in the audience. Mess up your capitals or commas and they'll happily point it out to you. You'll look less professional and as a result the the punctuation police will tut in your general direction.

- If someone asks you a question and you don't know the answer, you will have four main choices of response. The first is to blag it like a boss. Make stuff up that sounds like you know far more than anyone in your audience and also make the person that asked the question wish that they hadn't. However this is a risky choice because of option two, which is to try and blag it and fail dismally. Get caught out with even the faintest whiff of bullshit at the risk of everything else you talk about having the same odour. Thirdly, you can apologise, cry a little, say you don't know and hope they don't see you crossing your legs. Fourthly, and by far the best option in any situation when you don't know the answer to something you've been put on the spot about, is to admit you don't know and say it with some conviction. That is not to say you're proud in your ignorance, but saying "I'm sorry, I don't know that" with confidence and conviction carries with it an impression of honesty that doesn't defile everything else that comes out of your mouth. It validates your self-assurance and knowledge in everything else you have talked about. None of us know everything after all, and few people will mark you down seriously for one small point when you're being straight with them.

Top tip: In life outside uni be careful not to take this point to the extreme though. "I didn't know I wasn't supposed to show you my hairy arse officer" said with conviction will likely earn you one.

Projects and working with other students

Many courses these days will expect collaborative work with others. Unless you're going to be a professional hermit there are few career choices that will allow for you working in total isolation. Thus having some basic skills in performing joint tasks with others, without leaving them with a feeling of homicidal intent towards you is a bonus. When you're initially given this piece of work the tutor will likely focus on the content of the project, however your gaze will, with most probability, be drawn to the oiks you've been saddled with.

If you're really lucky you'll be partnered with some well adjusted, focused, driven and helpful individuals who want to take a balanced approach to your project, divide the tasks out according to strengths, and want everyone to maximise their potential. Meanwhile back on Earth, your group will consist of none of the above.

What you will have however is a combination or all of the following:

- The procrastinator. They'll take a back seat to the proceedings with the intent that if they can keep quiet enough the work will somehow just go away. They can't wait to get away and by the time you have your final group meeting they'll either need to be carried or have quit the course already.

- The neurotic. They will desperately want to control the proceedings, laminate everything and, if you're really unlucky, give you a name badge. There's most likely some premature midlife crisis going on in the background that will somehow find its way into the proceedings. Everyone else *will* be organised, whether they like it or not, to their schedule.

- The joker. Your meetings will be golden and irresistible opportunities for impromptu stand up and no subject will be off limits. These people are an unhealthy (but fun) distraction. Hide their amphetamines.

- The mum. In all likelihood a mature student, who reminds you all, with timely precision, how her kids are all your age or older. Her catch phrase will be something akin to "yay team!"

and she's going to bring biscuits. She may want to do a little bit of your work for you and if you're quiet enough you might just catch her saying "bless" under her breath. However get her drunk and watch the transformation from fluffy maternal to the emotionally starved cougar that just won't get off your lap.

- The rabbit. So named because of the perpetually frightened *car headlights are approaching fast!* look on their face. You could tell them to do your work, because the rest of the group had a meeting in their absence, and this was decided. They will do it. This person is the primary candidate for being forgotten about until the last meeting when someone asks where the worried person is who's name you can't remember.

- The intellectual. Prepare to feel inferior. This project that you and your colleagues are dragging out is only slowing their imminent Masters degree and PhD. They'll probably wear a tie and be grateful for any invite to any social occasion. You might just accidentally find out you're their new best friend if you're not careful.

- The socialite. When not updating her level of boredom on Facebook, her only likely contribution is going to be something akin to "woohoo!" as the meeting concludes so she can go "partaaay" with her friends, just assuming she can get through the door with those gigantic hoolahoops attached to her ears.

Remember that the hardships of a group project are limited. Perform well or terribly as a group, but remind yourself that this is only temporary. Make the best of who you have and don't use the others as the excuse that you are failing. Succeed in all your other areas of your study and this part of your course will have minimal impact if it all goes pants.

Additionally, having a semi-dysfunctional team of individuals that look like they have more in common with a medieval freak show does in actual fact reflect real life. Only in Hollywood movies do teams of people gather who are all well adjusted and perfectly balanced against one another. Reality, in the professional world, will have you making do with people who are as well matched as clown shoes and country hiking.

Plagiarism

If anything is going to get you nailed to the vice chancellors door, this is it. Plagiarism is the act of taking someone else's idea and including it in your work as if you came up with the idea all by yourself. Amongst academics, intellectual theft is akin to cannibalism. Hence the very strict rules with referencing to death any written piece of work. The assumption is that anyone studying at undergraduate level is still incapable of independent ideas that hold any serious value.

Plagiarism also covers copying other students work and presenting it as your own. These days you can pull an essay off the internet quite easily, but there are now computer programmes that scan thousands of pieces of work in order to catch out those who plagiarise. So don't copy from your mates either. Note that you can also plagiarise yourself, and they will do you for this as if you copied directly from the lead text on the subject. This might seem a bit odd, but what they don't like is you taking apart an old essay you wrote and reconstructing it as a new piece of work. If you're going to use some information you already used in a previous essay don't go to town with the copy and paste facility on your computer; break it down and rephrase it.

Work placements

Some courses offer placements as part of the qualification. This means that you might be required to go out in to the big wide world and work/study outside the safety of the campus gates. You might be expected to enter the workplace and put in some hard graft before you even get a job. For some this will be quite daunting and for others it will feel like you're half way there with your chosen profession. Either way, the best tactic with this is to get stuck in and give it your all. One of the potential pit falls with being a student is that many people have the impression that real life will be totally on hold for three years. Whilst uni life should include some serious fun and frolics, you can't always take this into the workplace. Turning up to your student placement on day one and smelling like you've just crawled out of a vat of gin is not going to be one of your better moments.

The expectation of many placement managers will be that you're there to work. The truth is you're there to work *and* learn. You are not a skivvy however you might be treated as such in many placement areas. If you complain you will only reinforce this attitude and there will always be some official reason why fetching the tea and biscuits is all part of the learning process. The best way to get through this is to suck it up and get on with it. Also the way to maximise your placement potential is to create a fuss and make every effort to become a human limpet to those who should be mentoring you. Ask questions and do your best to make them feel good about their work. Statements such as "this work place is all a bit crap, isn't it" won't earn you their affection and will only serve to take them one step closer to a box of antidepressants. Take the most boring, drained, overworked and disheartened person in the world, then take a genuine interest in who they are and be enthusiastic about their expertise, and you'll find they'll be more energised and keen to share to your advantage. If you reinforce their negativity you may as well go ahead and jump off the roof together.

> *Top tip: Turning up late doesn't make you fashionable and arriving half cut might make you fun, but the dole queue is not.*

The university staff

There are many employees of the uni including the behind the scenes staff and all of those who are there to help facilitate the smooth flow of your higher education experience. Most of these people don't get paid a fortune for the hard work they do, so make sure you don't treat them like the turd that won't flush. Many put in long hours and have to deal with all sorts of rubbish thrown their way before they get to their brief encounter with you. Additionally, in any interactions in your future workplaces, you will learn at your peril the hazards of treating disrespectfully those that you rely on for minor services. Being friendly, polite, patient and respectful to people might unfortunately scar your hard worked image as a hooligan, but you'll find that things run much smoother academically. So be polite and communicate with your lecturers and tutors in a warm manner. If you're having difficulties, then letting them know that you're taking your studies seriously will earn you help, and what you're studying is after all their life's work. So be nice.

The academic staff will likely be your main point of interaction with uni personnel. Whilst the above rules apply it does you in good stead to have an overview of differing styles and personalities with your tutors:

- The too cool for school tutor. He or she will pretend to flaunt the curriculum and are easily led off topic. They will want to dress more like you than their colleagues and will have little use for chairs, often preferring to perch on top of the nearest table. They tend to fancy themselves as academic hipsters. Their hair will be snazzy and their attempted use of modern slang will probably be twenty years outdated, but they will still try to get down and be hip with the rest of you. Their jokes (and there will be many) will be somewhat amusing at first, but hold on in there. At the moment they think you're sniggering at them rather than their quick wit then they can and will drop into formal arsehole mode.

- The midlife crisis tutor: Over-familiarity will be obvious to everyone else but them. Sad people needing affection, who are also in a power position, find it hard to conceal their thoughts. Beware of social media invites or references to what a party animal they indeed are (in the hope of an invitation). Also be prepared for plenty of poorly concealed references that relate more to their ex-wife than the subject being taught.

- The traditionalist tutor: The mild aroma of pee drizzled tweed and elbow patches are the garments of choice with this one. Bifocal glasses and pipe smoking are also distinctive hallmarks of the trade. If you need to leave them a message, it's best pinned to their office door, as computers will be thought of as inherently evil. Email them at your peril. And boys that wear makeup will be thought of as girls.

- The politically correct tutor: He/she/it will mark

you down if you are suspected of, in any way, being non-PC. They don't see things in black or white, including common terms of reference. There will never be a black or a white board in their classroom. There will be a *marker* board (unless of course Mark might be offended). Political correctness is not dead, nor is it living impaired.

- The control freak tutor: Whilst organised, punctual and thorough, be careful not to get between them and their well timed lecture plan. This type is only one small step away from a swastika and a motivational three hour speech about student responsibilities. DO NOT request an essay extension without wheeling your deceased granny's corpse in with you.

The academic side of university is in reality quite hard work if you do it properly. You will have three or four years to knuckle down and get to know a profession or subject really well. Remember you're aiming at becoming an expert in you chosen field of study. Whilst the uni bar and all of the other distractions are great fun, please beware that there are those that leave uni with about as much knowledge in their chosen field as someone who caught half an hour of it on the Discovery Channel. There is a huge gap between a first class honours degree and a scrape through result. Employers will know by your final grade whether you're the sort of work hard until the job is done type of person or whether you probably spent more time in three years of study lazing about in your underpants.

Chapter 4: Accommodation

One of the most liberating aspects of being young and going to university is the realisation of freedom you get when you enter your accommodation. For many people at 18 years of age, the first term could possibly be the longest period spent away from mother and father dearest. It's a wonderful and exciting feeling seeing your tiny, poorly ventilated and dingy toy-box of a room that would give most hamsters claustrophobia, but to the average fresher on day one, the only thing missing is a sign nailed to the door with the inscription "welcome to the love palace". The feeling of freedom will, for some, be accompanied by small pockets of self doubt and anxiety, but don't despair as within a few days this will in most likelihood pass, in exchange for excitement and growing confidence borne from independence.

There are two main choices (if you're lucky) for your digs when starting uni. Well, there is also a third, but this one isn't worth contemplating: you can always attend a uni that is close to your parents place. You may tell yourself that this will save you some rent money and at least you can get your washing done. The cost to your social life though will be horrific. Also the real rationale for this choice is more likely to involve co-dependency issues with you and your parents and for this reason alone you should move out and go further afield. The two sensible options are firstly, opting for accommodation on campus, or secondly, getting your own digs off campus. There are both advantages and unfortunate consequences to either decision, but whichever you chose at least you're not still stuck to the teat at home like a minority of new students. And if you are one of the home birds, I suggest you keep your options open, be honest to yourself as to your motivation and consider uni accommodation as at least a possibility for the future.

Life on campus (or nearby in uni owned students halls) initially requires you applying in good time for a room. Therefore planning in advance and a little of bit of organisation and form filling are required. Leave this to the last minute at your own peril, because there will be a shed load of other students doing the same and if you don't get it in on time your options will rapidly become very limited. However, having completed the forms in good time you will hopefully be awarded a place of honour in one of the luxury five star halls of residence the uni has to offer. A word of advice: don't pack like you're never expecting to return. Leave the houseplants and the family dog where they belong or at least just for the time being. When you get to uni and see that all written here is misleading fabrication then you can send the butler back home for the other furniture to deck out the west wing.

Once you arrive, most organised people will want to unpack and find a home for all their stuff, which makes good sense. Getting all this done on day one will keep you busy and focused for a short while which is a good thing, especially if you're pining for home or feeling apprehensive. Also keep your door open whilst you're at it, as other students might feel more compelled to pop in to say hi if they see you squirreling away. If you choose to live out of a suit case like a hobo, the chances are you'll soon start to look like one. Get your kit out, hang stuff up and get your clothing tucked safely and nicely away in wardrobes and drawers. It might not be long before one of your fellow students discovers what drinking more than two pints feels like, loses their self control and charges into your room at four in the morning with a foam fire extinguisher. From personal experience my old roommate and I can tell you the result being that everything not hidden away gets that lovely Christmassy festive feel.

> *Top tip: Some students feel the need to acquire small pets. Please develop a resistance to this urge should it arise. Hamsters or gerbils are attractive in pet shop windows and all the girls may find them cute initially. A hamster with a pungent dose of the trots and a failure to change its bedding might give your housemates homicidal thoughts.*

The facilities

If you're really lucky there is the possibility that you might get a room that has more furniture in it than a bed with a mattress infused with the faint odour of sweaty bodies and who knows what else. Some universities offer en suite facilities, however let's assume for a moment that you're not related to royalty, then at least your expectations ought to allow for some cut corners in the architectural designs. But look on the bright side; it's apparently more fun in steerage anyway, so chin up, man up and make do. My first room at uni consisted of something to sleep on, something to write on, a sink and a wardrobe that was half built into the room next door. Its dimensions we're half the size of my modest bedroom back at home so things felt a little squashed.

My roommate felt the same. It was fortunate we got on well as we didn't have much privacy. Put it this way, as you awoke each morning you damn well made sure you opened your eyes *before* you swung your legs out of bed, or god only knows what you might brush against. If you weren't careful you could instigate a very personal encounter purely by accident. Privacy is a luxury that will not as easily be achieved as you might be accustomed to back home. There just might be a moment of horror in the next year when you accidentally catch a waking glimpse of your roommate's nadgers. Not nice. Don't say you weren't warned.

The other potential problem with halls is that you are often required to share facilities such as the kitchen, toilets, showers and baths. This is no problem if you happen to be a total slob and are prepared to wait with siege like patience until someone simply does your washing up when they get hacked off with the stink and mould growth. On the down side, if you have any moderate level of decency, it can be a bit frustrating trying to use the kettle when someone else has been using it to steam the grease off their bike chain. Sharing fridges with a bunch of people you didn't choose to live with can be a bit of a pain too. Finding your empty pizza box on the kitchen side, following one of your housemates arriving back at the halls last night with a severe dose of the munchies can be a tad annoying. And as for unsupervised beer left alone in the fridge... You might as well entrust a flare gun to the local arsonist. Money is a precious commodity to most students, so a mildly inebriated student who sees the unguarded house fridge as fair game after midnight is not unheard of.

Top tip: Lead by example. If you clean the bath after you, so the person following doesn't have to scrape off an inch of your filth with an industrial sander, they might just do the same.

Off campus

Many first year students are encouraged to try and get into student halls. This takes away much of the apprehension of moving somewhere new where you don't know anybody. An additional incentive (and bonus for the general public) is that in ghettoing all of the newly arrived party animals away together, the university hopes that you and your neighbours are likely to have at least some level of tolerance of each other. You can party hard through the night until sparrow-fart on a week day and the rest of the working non-student population will stand a chance of getting some sleep. Trust me in that I've done the student thing of staying up to the early hours with a bunch of friends, making more noise than ought to be physically possible, whilst taking a stab at trying to drink more beer than a boatload of thirsty Vikings. If a bunch of noisy, raucous students moved in to the house next door to me right now I'd expect to be polishing my new shotgun within the week.

Living off campus can sometimes be both a good and healthy thing to do, however there are some important considerations that ought to be made with the house share option. Before we get to that though, the other possibility with off campus accommodation in your first year is that you might need to simply rent a room from someone. I know a few people who did this (late applications LOL) but know of no first year students that even remotely enjoyed the experience. If you've already arranged this then you might well be the exception to the rule, however in my experience, most first year students want to spend this part of their lives behaving like first year students. Private landlords who rent out single rooms tend to get a little bit defensive when they wake up to find that your traffic cone collection in their front garden has gained yet another piece to add to the gallery overnight. They might also take offence to your mates wanting to come around at three in the morning to watch their boxed set sitcom series with you because they're bored. Some private landlords letting a room also have expectations of when

you are allowed to come and go. I remember a friend
who always had to leave campus early in the evening
for fear getting locked out. They also might not take
kindly to coming home from a hard day's work and
finding you slobbing out on the couch in your pants
with the remnants of last night's curry spread over the
coffee table adding interesting fragrances to the lounge.
Don't get me wrong in that there are definitely some
really wonderful landlords out there that you'll click
with and I was lucky to find one in the year after I
finished uni, however I feel this is a rarity so be careful.
Imagine what your grandparents would make of some
of your friends having to rent a room with them.

The house-share is frequently the better option for most
students living off campus. Again there is safety in
numbers. Many second year students are actively
encouraged to take a house and live off campus which
is something you can try and organise with your friends
towards the end of the first year if desired. So when
choosing your house have some consideration of the
location in which you are renting. If you opt to live 15
miles out in the sticks, away from the uni campus, you
might find yourselves a bit isolated. There are plenty of
rural villages where the bus service is not about what
time of the day the number 35 is expected, but what day
of the week it usually comes. Also if you choose a
rented house right next door to the local old folks
retirement village, expect to have the fuzz knocking on

your door any time someone with an intimidating haircut comes to visit. Ideally, if you can get a house-share somewhere not too far from where the uni campus is, then you're on to a winner.

Landlords renting to groups of students are a special consideration. Should you go and see a reasonable place that appears moderately tidy at a cheap enough rent but your gut is telling you that the landlord is a bit of a Muppet, then I'd be inclined to follow your instinct. Your intuition is an incredibly powerful and underrated tool for sniffing out danger and the occasional manipulative toss pot, so go with it when those internal warning bells and your spider senses start tingling. There will be obvious visual clues, such as his string vest displaying remnants of last night's dinner or the pit bull snarling at you. Listen out for the warning signals too. Ask him about the previous students he had in. Does he spit and grimace when he refers to what a delightful bunch of young people they were? Would he be prepared to share a phone number of theirs so you can reference him? If he's a quality landlord he's unlikely to start spouting the Data Protection Act at you or claiming he lost their records. Landlords always keep basic contact details of the people they have, just in case they need to contact them to request the spare key they accidentally departed with, where the bath plug is, etc. If he's a complete arse there's no way in hell that he'll want you phoning a previous tenant. If it looks like bullshit and if it smells like bullshit, guess what? So don't be intimidated. They want your business just as much as you need a place to stay. Take a good look around the place and sleep on it if you're not sure.

When it's time to sign the rental agreement take care to have a good read over the document. It's amazing what crap you might be liable for if the landlord wrote it himself. Many rental agreements are bulk standard and some private landlords will go through letting agencies for this too. Make sure you pay attention to the details and the list of contents. When it's time for you to move out and the landlord is asking you where the Picasso is you'll be glad of this simple check. Also if you find on closer inspection that your enthusiasm clouded your judgement when you signed the agreement and you didn't notice the leaking roof or that the back bedroom is being used as a crack den, then get on the blower to the landlord ASAP. Gather evidence: take photos, cross reference the rental agreement, document when you attempted to call the landlord or which agent you spoke to and if you need to send letters or death threats then keep copies. This puts you in a powerful position if they turn out to be negligent. Some people don't expect students to stand up to intimidation so, when necessary, getting all formal on their arse will put that one right.

On the flip side, please remember that the landlord is a real person, with real feelings and poops just like everyone else too. So don't destroy their business by negligence and carelessness with their property. If you break it then replace it or cough up the cash to cover it. And if you and your chums accidentally set fire to the sofa then tuck your collective tails between your legs to go apologise and own up together.

Housemates

If you're lucky there will be some choice on your part before you arrange a house-share, however for many first years it's simply a matter of being lumbered with whoever you're given. This can be fun and also helpful in that you'll end up mixing with others who you otherwise might not have bothered with. You could gain some wonderful friends who will have a lasting impact on you for the rest of your life. You could also find some who take the concept of slacking off and self depravity to a whole new level. Watch out for the following:

- The borrower. Not as in the vertically challenged movie, but the type of house mate who starts out with simply asking "can I just..." or "you wouldn't mind if I just borrowed..." Lend this person money and you will see it again one day, just as soon as you get some really good blackmail on them that would otherwise result in time served at Her Majesty's pleasure. You may as well simply take your bank notes, wrap them in bacon then toss them in the air in front of the neighbour's dog and still have more luck of getting recognisable currency returned. The alternative for the borrower type returning cash is the unsaid expectation, on their part, that they can return your money lent with kindness instead. There may come the day when they give you a hug and remind you that they're there for you when you need them (unless of course you need that 20 quid back in a hurry). Another common method of pay back, when you approach them for the return of the loan, is to swear blind that they gave you your money late last Saturday night just before closing time (can't you remember?). Whilst payment by magic is more commonly associated with the students on the wizardry module, they will insist that you were not in fact visiting your poorly granddad like you thought you were, and your twin did actually gratefully receive the cash, therefore debt repaid. Furthermore they lent you an extra fiver and can they have it back now please? The borrower of cash is also biologically a close relative of the impulsive borrower of stuff. Be careful to lend them that new CD you just bought. They will never try and tell you they no longer have it or attempt amateur hypnosis in an effort convince you it was already returned. Their tactic is far more subtle and clever. They will look you in the eye, smile and say something along the lines of "oh silly me, I keep forgetting, I'll bring it back next time" etc. You may as well go and buy yourself another CD.

- The emotionally insensitive. This classification of housemate is not a bad person, albeit just one small step away from psychopathy. It would in fact be far easier to deal with them if they were. With bad people you can simply say "sod off, I don't want anything to do with you" and the boundaries are clear. The emotionally insensitive however are only truly understood by their own kind. This is the type housemate who will place their full cup of coffee on your closed laptop on the table in front of you. They'll guff loudly in front of your new girlfriend when she's visiting the house and become openly offended when they don't laugh. They'll also explain to her that you and he have farting competitions each morning, and that everyone can normally hear you parping loudly from the bathroom all the way in the lounge. They'll answer your phone that you foolishly left on the kitchen table and explain to your tutor calling that you're busy taking a dump.

- The emotionally oversensitive. When this type

of student starts to become emotionally dysregulated you and this side of campus will know about it. They are usually female however this is not exclusive. If she is your girlfriend, well good luck with that one. Don't forget her birthday, pet's name, favourite colour, dress size (minus two) and whatever you do, don't see her best friend as fair game when she dumps you periodically. You won't be dumped (like she said you were) but will in fact be having a trial separation or break. Before you know it the main conversation amongst those in the uni bar will be your total lack of sensitivity, disgusting belching habits and penis size (minus two). If however she is not your girlfriend and you are simply seen as a minion then your supportive role will be more relaxed. There will be an expectation that she can call you at four AM for a teary chat about her git of a boyfriend and will make you promise to tell everyone you meet in the next 24 hours about what a loser he is. She will more than likely be in a new relationship with the next unfortunate in a week's time and the game starts all over again.

- The gossip. A well timed anonymous call to this person, letting her know the TV licensing van has been spotted, and within half an hour hundreds of students will be cutting the plugs off their TV's (true story by the way). If you want to quickly pass a message to the entire student body simply start a conversation with the word's "don't say I told you but..." then sit back and watch the magic unfold.

- The model student. This is the person we all at one point hoped we might turn into, usually when buying our first academic text, which incidentally is now propping up the wonky cooker in the kitchen. They will somehow have managed to hold on to the motivation to get all of their essays started well before they are due and will have read all of the key texts. They might even begin to have a crack at the first draft of their dissertation. I recall meeting a guy who in his first year showed me a hand written draft copy of his first attempt at writing an academic book. He was also a really nice bloke who went on to achieve a first class honours degree. Git. Good to have as a house mate in some respects, especially if the rest of you are challenged in the health and hygiene department.

- The Casanova. This guy could fall in shit and still smell of roses. He's not the brightest of God's creatures however his IQ is not his main survival mechanism. He'll score well enough academically, just as long as he gets a middle aged female divorcee tutor marking his work who he can smile at as he sits at the front in lectures on the one or two occasions that he chooses to attend. His social calendar is busier than Heathrow at Christmas. He will also taunt the rest of you mere mortals with the frequency in which you find nubile young fillies wandering around the house first thing in the morning wearing nothing but his t-shirt and boxer shorts whilst eating your cornflakes. Never, ever use his towel in the bathroom. And pray he doesn't use yours.

- The geek. Academically this person performs well. They know their way around a computer and if you ever need help fixing your laptop they will be more than happy to assist. Beware however that you may be required to feign an interest in dragons or make a public display of fake enthusiasm regarding their new cat themed website. This is easily achieved however as emotional intelligence is not high in their skill set and if there is the briefest flutter of insight that you only want them for their laptop fixing abilities then you can offset this with a simple party invite. They will never show up but the offer will work better than the Jedi mind trick. Try and be nice though; they are a delicate flower and abuse their trust too much or take the piss out of their Klingon dictionary and you might just find your Facebook profile locked down and your face pic replaced with a baboon's arse or worse.

- The party animal. Approach with caution. This nocturnal beast will, if you are not careful, whisk you away faster than a turd in a log flume. Whilst the experience will no doubt be something to treasure, if you happen to have exam revision or an essay due, reassurances of "you can always study tomorrow" might seem appealing however are not truly based in reality. Study and hangovers don't sit well together, especially if you wake up in a different county. I remember a guy who went for a night out in the city and woke up 50 miles away with no recollection as to how he got there.

You will soon learn that with a house-share there are some essential responsibilities that you all have. There are certain practical aspects of living together that you will need to adhere to, and number one on this list is that you never, ever run out of bog roll. The moment this happens, you may as well be living in the woods. Having a central fund for certain basics that you throw a fiver into on a weekly basis might pay dividends. Additionally having a cleaning rota may sound dull, but it will assist in keeping the local vermin at bay. Avoid that bombed out graveyard look and keep to the schedule.

> *Top tip: your landlord may try and*
> *convince you that when you signed*
> *the rental agreement he has the right*
> *to use you as his personal body slave*
> *for the year. Keep the rental*
> *agreement safe as it will also include*
> *details about his responsibilities.*
> *When the boiler packs up in February*
> *you don't have to survive by burning*
> *your course work and wearing*
> *everything you own.*

Unity

When you arrive in your lovely new accommodation, whether this is a house on or off campus, you should make a concerted effort to get along with those who you are living with. Many shared houses will opt to go out for a house meal, a few drinks or both in an attempt to get to know one another. Take this opportunity to try and get to know, and more importantly, get along with your fellow students. These are, after all, the people you will be sharing with for the next year (until they lock you out, of course) and if you want someone to give a monkey's about cleaning up after themselves, they are more likely to do so if their mess would otherwise impact on someone they like.

Be prepared for a little light hearted madness though. Some houses are settled havens of academic purpose, whereas others may be a little bit on the unpredictable side. I recall walking in to one house in my first year and to find a cacophony of music, shouting and laughs emanating from the building. Inside there was someone riding a bike through the corridors and wielding a ketchup smeared tampon as a weapon whilst his housemates ran for cover. This was the norm for this place. Someone was handcuffed naked to the railings on another day and I also heard a story about someone who had their room key stolen when they were in the shower. Someone with long arms had then reached through a top window and glued it to the inside of a lower part of the window. The unfortunate victim had to call out campus estates management while dressed only in his towel in order to get him back into the room. I also heard another story where a friend turned up at his house to find the front door locked from the inside. He was given a message through the door to post his trousers through the letter box before they would agree to let him in. Foolishly but seeing no alternative he eventually did as requested leaving him stood in the street for some time in just his skiddies.

Practical jokes are frequently part and parcel of being a first year, and whilst these silly antics can sometimes land you in a heap of trouble if you're not careful, what would uni life be without a little silliness? My roommate and I enjoyed taunting some of our fellow student housemates in our first year however we also had our fair share of pranks played back. My room keys went missing one day and I was convinced I'd simply misplaced them. How were we to know that our next door neighbour in our house had got them? As we walked back from the pub that night we laughed at the sight of someone's whole room having been transplanted and left outside in front of the house including beds, kettle, books and even the posters of scantily clad women. We laughed right up to the point when we realised it was our stuff, however in a bid to salvage the pride we slept outside rather than feel beaten. I awoke first thing to people laughing, taking photos and commenting at what a couple of freezing cold plonkers we were. In all fairness we had water-bombed our neighbour on her way to lectures the previous day and she did take it reasonably well. I remember another occasion when we stole a friend's prize teddy bear that she'd had since a baby. We posted her a heavily accented voice recording that any self respecting terrorist organisation would have been proud of, threatening bodily harm to the teddy unless our demands of several pints were left in the uni bar by a particular time. She got her own back.

The housing feud is another interesting and not uncommon game, where two houses go head to head in humiliating, winding up or just generally being annoying to the other house. This is one of the funniest games you'll ever see on campus and when it all kicks off it can happen in style. I recall a story about one house going out for their traditional end of term fiery curry, which is of course accompanied by a shed load of beer. Whilst out the rival house broke in and removed all of the toilet doors from the stalls. Not pretty, but ingenious all the same.

The list of stories is almost endless but the message is simple and brief. Have fun. Not so much at the expense of all else but remember that being a student (especially in your first year) is also about living. There is a time to work and you know the rest, but just make sure any prank you play on someone else is less than what you'd be prepared to take yourself.

> *Top tip: One final word on accommodation. Invest in a roll of duct tape and some screwdrivers. Shit breaks.*

Chapter 5: Health and Wellbeing

Looking after yourself involves more than just being able to handle yourself in a pub brawl. It's about hygiene. It's about soap and water. It's about taking care of the basics without the necessity of mum behind you nagging you to wash behind your ears and change your underpants once every new moon. For some people personal hygiene is nothing more than a quick spray of some cheap and dodgy aerosol that will floor the average asthma sufferer at 30 yards. This chapter will cover a few of the basic dos and don'ts including some common problems that many people will face...

...and starting with faces, don't forget to wash it and also brush your teeth, stinky pants. Regular cleaning is not only something to do when you're on a hot date, but should be built into your daily routine. This may sound patronising but when left to your own devices in this world, without mum doing your washing, and with you actually having to buy the odd bar of soap yourself, there is the potential for some students to allow things to slip a little. And when things start to slip with personal care, it's not long before your dirty skiddies are being recycled well into double figures and the wash sink in your room becomes an unofficial personal urinal to rival any inner city underpass. Also make sure you shower with reasonable frequency. Wash behind most things and under the rest, and you can't go far wrong.

Another interesting and unusual fact about young blokes going off to uni for the first time is that there is going to be no one there to do your washing. "Ah ha" you may think. "I've got/ am going to get/ will pay someone else's girlfriend to do this for me. After all, mum's a girl of sorts isn't she, and she's always washed my skids."

However shocking as it may seem, what might appear to be a natural and inborn ability to operate a washing machine is not actually built into the female genetic code. When I first met my wife she kindly offered to do some of my washing, (that's the way I seem to remember it, however for the sake of argument, somehow my washing ended up in her wash bag) and it never came back quite the same. My favourite, old, knackered and much loved winter jumper looked like it has been used as the piss mop in the local gent's after a busy Saturday night. She's much better at operating the washer and drier now, however only at a trade off for the ironing. She doesn't turn my clothing pink and I don't try and iron her silkies on the top heat setting anymore. An interesting little technique worth learning: place one of your arms in the air above your head. Now bend your elbow and bring your hand down slowly towards the back of your head. Slide your hand down the back of your neck and into the top of the clothing you are now wearing and you will find a funny little bit of your clothing that feels slightly rougher or coarser than the rest. Think of this unusual artefact as *the label* and on it is embedded a secret code on how not to turn stuff pink.

There's a good chance that your campus will have an odd little out of the way building/room that serves as a clothes washing place. The technical term for this is *the laundry*. This is the room where you can put money in a machine, stick your nasty skiddies in there and it all comes out wet but clean by the time you've sunk a few pints. Don't leave it too long and get carried away in the bar though, unless of course you want to find your prize pair of veteran tighty whities unceremoniously dumped on top of the machine to make way for someone else's washing load.

There are usually driers close by. If you've not used

one of these before, the golden rule for not setting shit on fire is finding and removing the fluff from the fluff catcher before you stick your stuff in there. There might even be an odd ironing board knocking about too. This makes stuff flat and not creased. The more technically minded and adventurous might like to set the standard and give all this a go. Alternatively you might just want to reinforce the trademark student fashion of having creased everything.

> *Top tip: If you only do your laundry once in a blue moon, having recycled your pants on both sides several times, you might have to spend what feels like an eternity to get it all done. Alternatively, do it regularly and thus making the laundry part of your weekly schedule will save you a lot of pain. Furthermore the quietest time to get to the laundry, when all of the machines will be free is late Friday night. :/*

The next bit of bad news is that there will be no one about to clean up stuff. In the past mum may have been about, to hang your coat up, when you just left it hanging over the back of the arm chair in the lounge, and somehow the skid marks left in the toilet pan manage to disappear before her next coffee morning with the neighbours, but now the game has changed. You will have to start planning your actions a little more carefully so that you don't find yourself buried under your own filth before the end of your first month. Cleaning stuff is unfortunately not the most pleasant job in the world but the good news is that as you're now officially a poor student, you probably don't own much, therefore have less to clean. Take that, rich kids! However, what you do have, you should probably make the effort to keep tidy. For one, girls don't seem to find sharing a coffee mug, because it's the only clean(ish) one in the house, that attractive. Vermin do on the other hand. When your house rubbish bin forgets to take itself out when full, and starts sprouting little baby rubbish supermarket carrier bags over the kitchen floor, it's time to start cleaning some crap up.

Another unusual fact, when many first come to uni, is the keenness in which some people want to start growing facial fluff. For some this is nothing more than a temporary fashion statement (or a public declaration of "look how much testosterone I've got"), however for many it's a clear indicator of an aversion to shaving foam. So when the urge rises to join the ranks of manly beardedness and you choose to take a stab at squeezing out more facial hair than a grizzly, don't neglect giving it the odd spot of shower gel. It's also easy to get food caught up in there, so if you're going to be a fungus face, checking it for foreign objects every once in a while is desirable. If you're going to make the effort to stay clean shaven though it's worth making sure you spend more than 30 seconds on your face in your rush to get to the bar. I recall seeing a young first year lad, fresh off the peg, walk into the common room one day. You could tell he'd obviously only just had his first proper shave this decade as he looked like he'd just done one with a lawn mower. Furthermore he'd not bothered to spend much effort on finishing the job properly, which was indicated by the steady river of blood flowing from his neck. He looked as if a biblical plague had got busy on his face. The simple lesson here is that if you're going to make an effort, make it more than a half arsed one.

Registration with local services

When you've arrived at uni, done freshers' week, got your digs sorted and are starting to feel a little more at home, something that many people don't really get around to until they absolutely have to is registering with a new or temporary GP. As you've moved away from home and will now be spending more time at uni than anywhere else, it might make sense to take five minutes to get down to your local GP surgery and register with them. That way, when you fall ill with a rash or dose of the nasties, all of your records from the old GP will already have magically transferred themselves over to the new surgery making life easier for you. They'll also give you a new patient check up, maybe squeeze your nadgers if you're unlucky, tell you to cough, and all that other important stuff, but remember it is for your benefit really (not just a giggle for the surgery nurses). Remember that your GP surgery is your primary point of care *when* you need it and you're unlikely to know when you're next going to come down with a dose of leprosy. You might also want to register with the local dentist. That way, when you're in need of a bit a personal torture, you can save time with already having taken the hassle out of the procedure.

Your local doctors and nurses are a useful source of information, help and support when you're left to fend for yourself in the big bad world, so don't be afraid to approach them. Put a bunch of polite, well adjusted and sensible young people together for the first time and you're bound to sprout a few medical anomalies after a short period of time. Ever heard of meningitis? Your GP surgery will also have access to help and advice including contraception, sexually transmitted diseases, alcohol, drugs, and various physical complaints. They are also your typical access point to mental health services. You may not need any of these things however your friends might, and occasionally at uni you need to pitch in and help each other out. Don't be afraid to seek advice.

Another resource that is a gold mine of useful knowledge and advice is your local Citizens Advice Bureau. There may be no need to ever contact this service whilst at uni however knowledge about what is out there can sometimes prove useful when you least expect to need it. It's also a well known fact (i.e. sod's law) that if you know about this stuff, you'll never need it, so better safe than sorry. There are also other useful telephone based services that you ought to be aware of, and one of the most important of these is the 111 phone service which is available in many parts of the UK to compliment the 999 emergency service. The idea being that if you fall ill or need medical advice you can call 111 (otherwise out of hours GP services) for non-life threatening services. They can also dispatch ambulances if needed, however if you just happen to have been stampeded by a herd of buffalo and are still looking for missing body parts, 999 would be the better choice of the two.

On top of this there are also other phone based help lines such as the Samaritans and various drug and alcohol advice lines. In fact there is a whole host of support out there and my point here is not list all of the national or local support available in order to help you avoid meeting the reaper a few years too early, but rather to simply provide awareness that there is plenty of support on offer when mum isn't available to pick up the phone. There will be posters and leaflets all over campus detailing all sorts of advice and support services both internal and external to the uni. There will also in most likelihood be a student counselling/advice service if needed. No matter how desperate or embarrassing the situation might be I guarantee they've heard it all before. Additionally, remember that the internet is not only a source of interesting ladies doing interesting things, but also a wealth of information and support.

> **Top tip: Get yourself on a basic first aid course. Knowing how to place your mashed roommate in the recovery position might just be a lifesaver one day.**

Physical fitness

Your personal physical health is important. Now you have hopefully reached the point in your life where you realise that you are not actually indestructible and don't quite possess the physical skill set of Spiderman. On the other hand, the chances are that if you're under 20, you most likely feel that taking care of yourself physically is something that old blokes need to worry about. The fact is however that for every lack of effort to stay in shape now, you borrow from your future self. Conversely, be good to yourself now and you will reap the rewards in the future. This is not to suggest that you join a gym immediately and never ever see daylight again, but some sensible fitness would be a wise idea. Some commonplace uni activities to consider:

- Racquet sports. You may have some vague ideas about wannabe tennis star fans mincing around some court, desperately trying to connect with the ball without making a pig's arse of it all. However tennis, squash, badminton, etc. can all be really invigorating and aggressive sports. As a means to keep in shape and to let out some pent up frustration don't rule these out. Your uni will very likely have facilities for free or at least on the cheap. There may also be clubs if you fancy giving it a bash.

- Football. Whether the fully fledged Sunday All Stars team or a weekly five aside kick about squad, this is a great way to make some new mates and keep in shape. Also there's frequently a social side to these teams so you may find yourself counterbalancing all the good work and fitness with time in the bar, however it's still a balance. You'll be in better shape than those that do nothing but polish the bar stools with their arses at every opportunity.

- Rugby. Sort of like football but with more class, less personal dignity, more injuries and more beer. Rugby as a sport can be gruelling. However walk on to that pitch in a bad mood and guaranteed you'll come off feeling 100 times better. Directly in proportion to the physical demands are the silly arse games you'll be expected to join in with afterwards. Walk into any uni bar an hour after any rugby match and expect to see 15 or so naked backsides charging it around the place with flames and sparks trailing. I kid you not. The infamous *Dance of the Flaming Arseholes* is such a funny sight to see, just so long as you're not the poor rugger bugger on the receiving end. Serious drinking games, boisterous songs and other frivolities are all part of the experience. Think of it as a game for real men played by big children.

- Golf. Really? Well, a long and frustrating walk around a golf course for several hours is healthier than sitting on your rump.

- Running. Again, loads of clubs. Can be done on your own. Free.

- Cycling. Low cost (you can buy cheap bikes pretty much anywhere) and not bad for the environment when you need to get down the shops. There are plenty of local cycling clubs all over the place if not already with the uni.

  Top tip: cycling home from the pub is not always the best way to stay in good physical shape. It's also not the best way to stay on one piece.

The list can go on and on. The idea is to get you thinking that there are endless opportunities to do fun and healthy stuff. It's amazing how many people have the notion that getting or keeping in shape is about paying a small fortune for the privilege of joining a local gym which is either full of people desperately trying to hide their figures or others desperately trying to appear casual whilst sporting their own Lycra covered demigod bodies.

Beware the link with some sporting clubs/societies and alcohol. Booze often has its place at uni, but if you join the rugby club don't say you weren't warned that you might spend the odd evening literally running around the campus bar in nothing but your socks with 15 or so of your mates singing *Yogi does it in the fridge, polar, polar bear*. And this is not an activity people tend to do sober. Team sports however are a great means to meeting others, plus social contact and affiliation is a good healthy thing for people too.

Mental health

This one can be so misunderstood and yet is so important to all of us. The most complex and vital part of your body is... Okay, the second most important organ you possess right now (as you aspiring medical students out there will know) is your brain. If you don't take care of your head, it doesn't matter what sort of fantastic physical shape the rest of your body may be in. The problem for most here is that they're often not aware that they have any mental health needs... as well, life and stuff sort of just happens and we deal with it, don't we?

People tend to shy away from mental health concerns. Even though there is better awareness today than ever before there is still a lot of stigma attached to anyone who might experience any sort of mental health problem, often borne out of misunderstanding and fear.

After all, doesn't Hollywood teach us that psychos wield the best axes and mad really means bad? The truth of the matter is that The Big Screen isn't the best teacher on this issue and even when it's trying to be sympathetic and understanding of mental health issues in the movies, it's frequently misdirected or at best misunderstood. An interesting truth for you is that you will already know people who have or have had some form of serious mental health issue, yet you've not been aware of it because they chose not to run it up the flag pole. Another basic truth is that people don't go about telling others about it simply for fear of being misunderstood or being labelled as *a bit bonkers*. Whilst things are getting better in respect to public understanding there is still a large contingency out there who think that being mentally ill, at some point, involves the use of putting your underpants on your head.

For many people, going to uni is the first time they are going away from home for a sustained period. There are all the potential worries including various social concerns. Have I made the right choice of course? Is this the right uni? Am I going to fail? Can I afford to go to uni? What expectations are being placed on me? Does this beard make me look like a garden gnome? etc. The list of potential concerns is endless and as such this can be a stressful time for people. But being in a new environment and not wanting to appear like the kid who wets the bed, people simply don't like admitting their fears; they get buried inside themselves and sometimes they build so much pressure that they have to pop in some way, shape or form. There are also the additional ingredients to the stress cocktail: drugs and alcohol.

This is a subject area that could be talked about in some finer detail but the most important point to get across, if nothing else, is to be sympathetic to those around you, especially when life gets a bit stressy. You don't necessarily know what people's backgrounds are and what they may have had to endure to get where they are. So not to harp on about this too much, here are some basic facts to consider:

- Psychotic does not mean psychopathic. Ever been in a crowded room with people talking or on the street in a public place and being convinced someone called your name? What actually happened was you misinterpreted another noise and your brain tried to make sense of it. Under the influence or not, that's interpreting the world in a slightly different way (albeit briefly) than everyone else. Go polish your axe.

- More bad stuff happens because of people who are not mentally ill.

- Just because you decide to wash your coffee mug more than once a fortnight doesn't mean you have OCD.

- People readily bandy about the word *depressed* without really meaning depressed. They usually mean *a bit low*. Clinical depression is in a whole different ball park.

- Just because someone may have a mental health diagnosis does not mean they are presently ill or indeed have been so for some time. So don't label and stigmatise people or treat them like they have a dose of the bubonic plague.

- Despite some popular media fantasies, bipolar disorder is not something trendy or to be aspired to. It's a condition where the sufferer gets sustained periods of being high and also long and unpleasant periods of being depressed. It is also something that many people manage very well with the use of medication and support but it's not nice for the sufferer when it hits. Just because you know someone who is a bit of a moody cow at times and a drama queen at others, it does not mean they have bipolar disorder.

- We ALL have a predisposition to some form of mental illness or other. Just add a sustained amount of stress to anyone and it'll happen. The difference is that unfortunately some have a greater vulnerability to stress than others.

- And as the saying goes: *just because you're paranoid doesn't mean they're not out to get you.*

In order to keep your mind healthy here are some hint and tips:

- Get some exercise. It has a positive impact on both body and mind.

- Don't hole up in your room. If you find yourself becoming anxious then changing your environment and getting out (go for a walk, join a club, explore campus, whatever...) is a very healthy thing to do.

- Do your best to live in the here and now. When people become overly obsessed with the past it can drag them down. If your mind is constantly whirring like a broken record, ruminating on the fact that you reversed over your granny's cat as you left for uni, then this can be a burden. When we have ruminatory thoughts we can't just switch them off (unless we have ready access to a shotgun - but that's a wee bit drastic). It can also be draining when our thoughts are constantly focused on the future. When we get obsessed with all the terrible things that might happen to us our bodies can start to throw us into a fight or flight effect. Essentially this is a normal response to abnormal circumstances. If you lived 2000 years ago it'd be perfectly understandable for you to scream like a banshee whilst trying to claw the eyes out of the beastie that just happened to jump out on you; otherwise pooping yourself and running away at the speed of a Grand National winner. Unfortunately in modern society man's automatic life saving responses can sometimes be triggered by less provoking events. Your self esteem is likely to go down the toilet pretty rapidly if you automatically void your bowels each time someone mentions the essay that's due next Friday. Therefore doing your best to bring your thoughts into the present as much as possible is a very healthy thing to do; and a great way to do this is by engaging with activities that stimulate your senses. Go for a swim, listen to some good music, join a pottery class, paint, whatever... the options are endless.

- Periodically give your body a break from anything that you really know is not good for you. Beer, cigarettes, Facebook, etc.

- Mingle with others. It doesn't matter whether

you join the debating society or make an effort to say hi to your neighbours. We are all social creatures, whether we realise it or not, and contact with other humans, as much as is reasonably possible is really healthy.

- Be honest with yourself if you find you are struggling. Speak to the uni counsellor. They don't bite very often and it's not a sign of weakness to talk to others. If you find that you start to lose interest in things, energy levels drop, your appetite disappears, you can't concentrate, your libido hits the floor and you start isolating for more than a few days then you might need help. Going to see your GP won't hurt. Younger people and especially men are particularly crap at seeking help or talking about it. Professionals won't judge you and the ability to seek some advice is a manly strength not a sissy weakness.

Diet

You are what you eat apparently. If this were entirely accurate I should be sporting a couple of hooves by now, however I do suspect there is some truth to the saying. The fuel we intake is what our body processes for its practical use. Therefore if what we consume with regularity every weekend is the nutritional equivalent to a plate of napalm with a side of poppadoms, then there really is no surprise when our body wants to fire it out with greater vigour than which it went in. Without your mum making you eat vegetables and refusing to let you soak your crispies in lager it may all be a bit too tempting to fall in to bad eating habits when you have to fend for yourself. So be warned and make some good habits early on.

To start with, beware of anything that offers itself as convenience food. The local burger joint may smell delicious and the fact that you only have to wait 30 seconds for them to launch it at you is appealing to many of us from time to time. Going there every day however will soon have you feeling sluggish and lethargic. Keep it up and eventually you'll need a fork lift just to make it to the front door. As a general rule of thumb, the faster the food you eat, the slower you are going to be. The majority of fast food places are unlikely to offer healthy, good and wholesome food choices and if they do it's more than likely to be on their kids menu or at a price equivalent to a three course meal bought from the local supermarket. What is convenient for your busy hectic lifestyle is unlikely to be convenient for your gut. I feel that we are generally more health conscious (if not practicing) today than 20 years ago, which is in a large part due to certain health campaigns and celebrity chefs doing their bit. However uni can so very easily be a fast food trap, especially if you have more social appointments that the Royal family.

Eatery places to avoid:

- Your local burger joint. Despite the promises of the latest mega fantastic value for money deal showing you a picture of a burger big enough to floor T-Rex, what you'll most likely get is unlikely to represent the advert from which you made your order. It's also probably going to feel just a bit too moist for comfort and chances are that if you ordered no cheese, it'll come with no pickle but enough cheese to send all of the rats in the bins out back into a diabetic coma. The staff here can also be an absolute charm to deal with. I remember hearing about someone working in one of these establishments who felt out of place in that they didn't have the same level of time served at her Majesty's pleasure as many of their co-workers.

- The local pub. If you're getting hammered and feel the need to order your next meal from the bar, you've either started the wrong way round or you've been there too long. Getting fed whilst you're out on the lash may feel like a sensible choice so that you're avoiding drinking on an empty stomach, but if you ate before you left you'd have it easier on your pocket and may also have eaten a better meal (hopefully).

- The kebab van. Oh my god! I refer you to the previous point about 999 services. But somehow magically delicious following a skin full of grog. Not to be eaten sober of course.

- Fish and chip shops. Okay, nice every now and again however I know places where they still fry chocolate bars, not only to feel they offer a novelty item but because people apparently order this stuff with some regularity. Some stuff just shouldn't go together. Chocolate soaked in batter infused hydrogenated fats with more trans-fats than a middle aged Rocky Horror performance. What more could a cardiac surgeon ask for?

- Your local pizza place. Apart from the small forest that was sacrificed to bring your pizza to you warm and boxed, there is also the dent it will make on your wallet as well as your waist size. This is my own personal nemesis and downfall however I urge others to consider just how bad pizzas really are for you. I could find you a load of statistics on this however I see little point in labouring a commonly known issue. For every pizza you eat, go and do 10 hours of pain in the gym and if you're Catholic add 20 Hail Marys because pizza truly is the devil's food. Only Satan himself would make something so bad for you taste so yummy.

Good food, good advice, goodbye

Go outside. Walk to shops. Find easy meals cook book for the culinary challenged (celebrity chef optional). Buy it. Walk back home. Open book. Skim read bits. Mark some recipes out. Decide what to eat over next few days. Go to shops. Buy food that corresponds to said recipes. Get hungry. Cook stuff. Eat it and don't die. Ta daaa! You can cook stuff to survive. Congratulations you're now an accomplished chef.

Anyone who claims that they can't cook really means that they can't whip up a Sunday Roast to sous chef standards. "I can't cook" (unless there is a genuine paranoid delusion involving kitchens) is simply missing three words: "be", "arsed" and "to". There are plenty of basic meals out there that take less that 15 or 20 minutes to prepare and make. It just takes a little practice to realise that this stuff is not rocket science and that most men are actually capable of doing more that cremating dodgy sausages on a BBQ whilst in a beer induced stupor.

Before arriving at uni it might make sense to go and

purchase a few simple items to help get you started. If you leave it until you've settled in, there is the distinct possibility that you may have already settled into bad habits of relying on the local fast food places and may be on your merry way to registering with the diabetic nurse. If on the other hand you're already kitted out to be more self sufficient, then you minimise the risk. Beware however that there is also loads of unhelpful advice from shops trying to sell you unnecessary stuff and they will persuade you that in order to make an omelette you need more high grade multiple steel folded and perfectly balanced sharp knives than a ninja could want for Christmas. And most people don't actually really need oven proof dishes made from a material designed by NASA for the space shuttle program. The simple truth is that you can most likely manage with a couple of pans, a single basic sharp knife, some cutlery and something to chop stuff on. The rest is mostly inconsequential.

What to cook is a matter of personal taste. That fact that you're cooking something for yourself rather than going for the fast food lard in a bun option is a good start. If you choose to be a little self sufficient make sure that you don't feel that this is you on a diet fit for hamsters for the next three or four years. By all means, if you want to go for the all-out health food option, and can make this work, then great, however with most people a reasonable balance is usually a more realistic and sustainable option. Remember the purpose of the advice here is to promote you employing a healthy *balance* that hopefully you are already used to, so that you don't get to uni and magically transform into an elephant seal overnight by falling into too many bad habits.

But... and this is a really *big butt* (*snigger, see what I did there?*) the most important fact to remember is that how you manage your self-care at uni is mostly about your personal choices. Take all this advice, take some of it or take none. What is essential is that *you* decide, otherwise it will feel like someone else's choice, and we all have a tendency to rebel against imposed authority. The best personal example I have for this is that I used to smoke, and it took me years to quit. The biggest (and only) block to years of quitting and starting again was my own mindset. I never realised how much I really hated others telling me "by the way, those things are really bad for you, think of the money and do you know what it does to your health, you ought to quit," which really translates into "I think you're a plonker". Not really motivational is it? The point here is not to lecture you on the dangers of smoking, but to lecture you on the hazardous emotional dangers of you not feeling in control of your own choices in life. True motivation comes from the conscious acceptance that you have freewill.

So you have your cook book, you have a vague idea of how not to die of starvation and now it's time to face my own very personal arch nemesis... The food shop. Oh how I hate thee! Now before we go on to *how to do a good grocery shop,* I just can't resist having a pop at the modern day notion of what shopping is. I don't mind food shopping when it's mooching off down to the local green grocer and then off across the road to the butchers, etc. However supermarkets are purposefully more convenient in many respects despite my acute hatred of everything they stand for. If there is a Hell awaiting me, Satan himself will be on a checkout asking me if I need help to pack my own shopping.

The foremost irritating things about supermarket shopping:

- Other shoppers. I generally consider myself a relatively optimistic and patient man. I do my best to be considerate of others and polite to people who I don't know. I rarely suffer road rage and in the various lines of work I've performed in the public arena I've patiently taken more abuse than should realistically be achievable in a lifetime. However cut me up with your supermarket trolley to beat me to the check out and you'd better hope I'm not packing in more ways than one. There have been many times, especially in a crowded supermarket, when I could easily have ended up as the local feature on the ten o'clock news.

- The staff. Why, oh why, are there always far fewer checkouts open than there are available staff. I've seen many a situation where there is one person operating on a line of 15 or so unmanned checkouts. The supervisor standing around appears oblivious to the stress this incurs and will be busy spending 10 minutes trying to arrange for someone else to make a tannoy message to get someone from stock taking in the warehouse to come to the front and open another till. In the time it took, the supervisor and tannoy operator could have managed the queue that's now built up to biblical proportions.

- The staff again. In particular the security guard at the front of one of my local stores. What a jobs-worth! Not that I'm trying to steal stuff mind you, but oh how my blood doth boil with his overt stares and scowling.

- The isles. Whilst not being the biggest fan of orienteering, I must eat up miles in shoe leather pacing those isles again and again looking for things. If I go to the supermarket for cheese, how is it that where the cheese used to live I can only find a special offer on a TV that I suddenly feel a compulsion to buy despite not needing a new one? Yet where the cheese has gone, who knows? It was in isle 23 last week but some clever bastard has decided to play hide and seek with my precious time and now I have enough food (because it was all on special 30 for the price of 29 offers) to cater for the local army barracks. Also where did this TV, a set of screwdrivers, car insurance and a new DVD come from?

- Christmas shopping. The equivalent to the famous Spanish Bull Run, but with far more blood and guts. Old ladies, that would otherwise be sending a small fortune to puppy rescue foundations and knitting jumpers with snowmen on, all of a sudden act more akin to homicidal maniacs with chainsaws. Every shopping trolley is a weapon to be feared. And once I've run the gauntlet and the misery is drawing to a close, I have a blissful end in sight only to arrive at the till queues of Purgatory. And why does the Muppet in front always take their time packing their freight lorry worth of shopping away? Eventually I'm at the front of the line. Patience is at an all time low by now and I can't wait to get out, so do I rush through like my arse is on fire? No! The bastard behind me can bloody well know what it feels like to be me. "No I

don't need help with my packing thank you."
I'll just plod along at my own speed and make
small talk with the cashier about the grotty
weather at this time of year whilst an artery on
the person behind me is starting to haemorrhage.
All is balanced in the world again.

- Self service checkouts. Is it only me, or does the
  phrase "unexpected item in the bagging area"
  and "please wait for assistance" make you angry
  enough to start fantasising you'd come shopping
  dressed as a suicide bomber?

Student shopping has some important differences to
"other people" shopping (i.e. those with steady jobs).
Firstly, students don't tend to have all that much cash.
However, take heed in that paying for your stuff with a
dodgy cheque that has more bounce than 80's soft porn,
won't earn you prizes with your bank. Some people can
walk into their local supermarket and buy their
shopping without too much thought, whereas students
have to be wise (you are the academic cream after all?)
with their purchasing. Shopping for your groceries
doesn't necessarily have to cost you a small fortune or
the need to resort to common thievery. Some tips:

- Shop in places where you know your shopping
  is going to be relatively cheap. If you put your
  snobbery hat on and shop in the most exclusive
  area of the city then expect to pay double for

half as much. However choose a more down to earth location and pay more down to earth prices.

- Be careful what you're shopping for. There are plenty of brands out there that will charge you double for the same stuff. Just because it's so shiny and lovely on the outside doesn't mean that it's quality on the inside. The opposite can frequently also be true though. Sometimes paying a little more for quality, especially in the case of fruit and veg, will lead to less wastage. You know this already however it doesn't hurt to remind you to shop wisely. Or conversely, a better message might be don't shop like a lazy arse.

- Go to the supermarkets at about 7 PM for some bargains. Around this time some of the bigger shops will start to price stuff down that will otherwise be beyond its sell by date the following day. You can really find some great deals if you're prepared to be creative. A word of caution however in that you may find yourself battling with the grannies out looking for the same deals... and going against a granny with a thirst for a bargain can be like a getting between a mountain gorilla and his prize banana.

- Learn to look at the labels. Just because it says sausage on the pack doesn't mean it necessarily is all sausage inside. You might find more meat on a butcher's apron.

- Shop with cash and leave your card at home, thus avoiding the temptation to impulsively buy a new wardrobe when all you went out for was sweet corn and potatoes.

- "Half price special offer" sometimes means, "buy this now 'coz it's now half the doubled up price it was last week. You mug" or "were you one of the Muppets who bought this stuff last week, when it was twice the price, thinking it was extra special because it was so expensive?"

- "Half price special offer" sometimes means, "this tastes like cat shit. Why did we bother to stock this rubbish?"

- "Half price special offer" sometimes means it's simply a promotional bargain item or because some pillock ordered too much. So think about buying more than you need right now but only for a well considered saving in the future. Well if it's cabbage that might not be a great idea but bog roll and deodorant have a pretty good shelf life.

- If you're sharing a house with friends, think

about consolidating your resources by cooking and shopping for each other. Consider it, don't necessarily do it. You might be shacked up with some tea leaf whose idea of honesty is to admit to spending only some of your house cash kitty at the pub on the way to the shops. Chavtastic.

Chapter 6: Alcohol and Illicit Substances

Booze

It's just too much to expect someone under the age of 25 to go off to uni and be completely sensible when it comes to a night out, whether this is in the campus bar or hitting the town. Additionally in the first two weeks of freshers' there is likely to be an expectation from your peers that getting hammered, in the most interesting ways possible, is the name of the game. The ability to legitimately get completely mullered is just too much to resist for the average student hitting the lofty heights of adult education for the first time. After all, for most young people, leaving home and going off to study somewhere miles away from their usual stomping ground induces both anxiety and excitement at the same time. It's hardly surprising why many flock to the uni bar in a mixed emotional state already under the influence of half a bottle of Dodgski brand vodka. And when you get there and you start to meet other people, you want to portray an image of yourself that will be lasting on the minds of those you meet; you'll want to present as both mature and fun at the same time. This frequently translates into mixed opposing behaviour involving showing others both how much booze your mature self can handle and also how fun you really are when pissed as a fart. It's therefore not really that surprising when events involving a huge amount of alcohol frequently become the social first port of call for many starting at uni. Furthermore it's not just the quantity of booze you can neck that's apparent, it also soon becomes about the ~~quality~~ variety of drinks you can down. Ask any student, the morning after their "totally amazin' night out" and you'll get tales of how many shots of X,Y and Z they necked in addition to all the other letters of the alphabet. There will however be less talk of how many *units* of alcohol they downed before vomiting over the campus sign.

The choice of venue is frequently the decision of the herd mind, however once confirmed there will be certain advantages and disadvantages alike to the setting. The most important factors to remember, when going out with a bunch of people who you don't really know yet, is to have fun (with them) whilst at the same time not making a complete tit of yourself. The place therefore is really a secondary consideration, however where you go will impact on what is acceptable behaviour and what will get you tossed out on your backside.

The campus bar

This is a safe haven for students. It's most likely not open to the general public, or at least it's not a place where non-student people will likely be offended by the antics of you and your fellow students. It is after all your bar and the expectation is that you'll be up to the sort of things that students get up to when feeling mischievous. However a word of warning: whilst difficult, it is actually possible to get yourself kicked out of such places. The boundaries may be a lot less tight, but urinate on the carpet and expect to be seeing a lot more of the outside of the bar in the near future. On the other hand most student bars expect a bit of overindulgence and encourage a party-hard philosophy by frequently being equipped with such necessary paraphernalia as the yard of ale and more methods in which to take more shots than an SS firing squad. The place will be designed with student antics in mind, including what goes on in rag week. It's not unheard of to discover such classics as the rag week male sale, drag beauty pageants, and other dodgy and humiliating party games going on (all in the name of charity of course), and the campus bar is the place where this sort of stuff usually happens.

As well as being adequately stocked, the campus bar will in most likelihood be staffed by other students earning a few extra quid whilst studying at uni. And as far as part time jobs go, this is the golden ticket if you have the need for a little extra cash and want to have a bit of fun whilst you're doing it. I enjoyed working in the campus bar so much that I (accidentally of course) ended up staying on a year after my degree to continue working in it.

One final word of warning/advice/general interest: the campus bar men's toilets are for some reason frequently considered free game for females to use as opposed to using their own. Additionally there always seems to be some happy couple doing what young couples do best when intoxicated in the toilets on any given drunken Saturday night.

> **Top tip: go for your dump before you leave your digs.**

The house party

The old classic socialising venue at uni is of course the house party. This is the time honoured university tradition of someone blatantly breaching the terms and conditions of their tenancy agreement in order to attempt to throw the mother of all gatherings in the comfort of someone else's property. House parties are occasionally lacking and dull affairs, however, depending on who sent out the invites, sometimes they can also be particularly messy and particularly fun too. You never know who's going to turn up and what's going to go down.

> **Top tip: when the police ask you nicely to turn the noise down, responses with the word "fascist" in the reply won't prolong the party atmosphere.**

Ideas for house party games:

- Anything involving a spinning bottle is always interesting, exciting, revealing or a bit of everything. Simply drink a bottle of whatever and arrange for people to sit around in a circle, make up some half baked rules about removing items of clothing, telling truths, doing dares, etc. and go spin. There are also numerous variations of this game involving playing cards. However, beware trying to fix the game in your favour. I remember trying this once, many years ago, and ended up having my boxers snatched off to be thrown out of the upper floor window, getting locked out of the room and having to do the walk of shame (in reality a cowardly run) downstairs and outside to retrieve them. It could have gone so much better.

- *Cheers to all those...* Classic game to play with a bunch of people, especially when the booze has been flowing for a period of time long enough for people to lose some of their inhibitions and normal levels of self control. The essential rules are that someone takes a turn to say "cheers to all those who..." and then follows this up with a statement or truth that others have to admit to (usually by standing and taking a drink). For example if I say "cheers to all those who came to this party in the hope of playing hide the sausage" and you were clearly seen sporting a pack of three rib ticklers earlier today, then you'd have to stand and take a drink. Everyone would know what a hopeful you are being and they all have a good laugh at your expense. However if you don't stand up, and someone blubs on you because they saw you in the chemist, then you get a forfeit (usually a whole pint). Let's just leave this one at that and hopefully everyone else will be more hammered than you and forget that you admitted to cracking one off in the campus library. (Any if you're reading this Mr *****, no, I haven't forgotten. Classic!)

- *The key game. (No, not that one!).* The key game with the string. Essentially two teams: boys and girls, with one exception per team, so the boys have one girl, and the girls have one boy. Both teams have a long piece of string and a key. The string on each team gets threaded down the shirts, tops, trousers, skirts, etc. of every team member and their one solitary girl or boy on the team has to thread a key along the string from one end to the other before the other team manage it. This can get a little bit gropey (if there is such a word) and there are obviously more risqué versions of the game as you might imagine.

- *Pharaohs.* One judge. Two teams, two victims. Lots of bog roll. Go! Forfeits for the losing team who fail to do the most thorough job.

- Another version of the Pharaohs game is with the same basic premise however, instead of toilet roll, you have your two teams split into males and females and they have to dress the victim (member of the opposite sex) in clothing items donated from the team members themselves. Cameras at the ready for this one.

- *Quick fire truth or dare.* Everyone sits in a circle. Start with someone who points at another player and gives them a dare or asks a question (with a yes or no response) that needs to be answered without hesitation. Hesitation earns a suitable forfeit. The victim then becomes the questioner. Unanswered questions or forfeits can be asked again.

- *Quick fire truth or dare with a twist.* The same basic principles but this time the questioner gives both a dare then the truth question at the same time. The victim has to drink while they think. Get to the end of the drink before a decision or answer is made and the dare has to be done.

- *The name game.* Another drink while you think game. Going round in a circle one person says a famous person's name. The person to the left has to say another name with the starting letter being that as the surname of the previous name. For example, I say someone's name with the initials DC, so you might respond with a name with the initials CF and the next says a name with the initials FA and so on. All the while drinking while you think. However say a name that is the same initial and the direction immediately reverses. So you said a name with the initials CF however the person to your left replies with FF, therefore it's your turn again. Obviously not the same name twice and if no one's heard of the name before a forfeit is earned.

- *Ibble dibble.* I've heard this one called all sorts however the basic principle is just the same. You have one wine bottle cork that is singed on one end with a lighter, or if you don't have a cork just use a marker pen, ink stamp, etc. Basically you need something that will leave a nasty and not too easy to get off mark from someone's face. Sit in a circle and go round giving everyone a number. If I'm number one I will start by saying "number one ibble dibble, with no ibble dibbles, gives this ibble dibble to number (choose a number) ibble dibble, with no ibble dibbles." I must then give the cork/pen/etc. to the person with the number I said and with no hesitations. Cock up/ stutter/ give it to the wrong person/wrong number of ibble dibbles/etc. and the team get to mark me on the face with the pen or cork. I now become number one ibble dibble with *one* ibble dibbles and this number goes up corresponding to the number of marks I get on my face. By the end of this game most people will have some marks however there is always one victim who looks like they just escaped from the local zoo.

- *Buzz*. This is a simple counting game with numerous variations. You start by replacing any number between one and twenty with the word "buzz". Essentially you go around the table taking turns counting quickly until you get to twenty with the one number chosen replaced with "buzz". Cock up and get a penalty. Get to the end and the person who says "twenty" chooses another number with a word/gesture/whatever and start again. For example you might choose to add a flipping the birdy at the barman gesture for number nine, and off you go again. If you cock up before twenty you take a forfeit and you all start the count again. The first few rounds are easy and then all of a sudden it gets quite complicated and messy.

- *Kings*. I've heard of this one but never played it, however it does sound fun. Essentially a drinking game with a pack of cards. The first person who gets a king has to choose a spirit, the next person to get a king decides what it's mixed with. The third to be dealt a king buys the drink and the last person of course is the unlucky bugger who gets to drink it. Obviously some weird and wonderful concoctions to be dreamt up with this one. Expect some sudden running for the toilet from someone after a short while.

- *Spoof.* Classic drinking game. Everyone gets three coins and then puts their hands behind their back to choose how many coins go in their right or left hands. Right hands then get placed on the table with everyone's left remaining closed. The idea is that everyone going around the table gets to guess how many coins are on the table (if there are seven players, each with three coins, obviously there will be between 0-21 coins). The same number can't be chosen twice. Guess the right number and you're out (which is a good thing). You then start again (and this time the maximum number of coins is going to be 18 because there are six players left). The idea is that the last person left has to down whatever nasty concoction is placed on the table at the start of the game. Alternatively every person that gets out has to add a portion of their own drink into the losers drink as they go out. Another rule is that you can call "spoof" at any time, which means you are declaring that there are actually no coins in the middle and that everyone has kept three coins in their left hands. Get it right and the remaining players all have to share in the nasty. Get it wrong and you automatically become the loser. Drink up.

- *Park bench.* Simple game. Two chairs together and one person sits on one chair. The next in turn has to sit next to them and then does whatever is needed to make them feel the need to move off (like someone undesirable sitting next to you on a park bench). They have 30 seconds to do it. Fail and there is a forfeit then the next person has a turn.

Finally and quite possibly one of the most interesting things you can arrange with a party is to make it fancy dress. That's not to suggest that everyone is given free reign though, as sometimes the best fancy dress parties are done with a planned theme. The classic toga party springs to mind. At the start of the evening everyone is all perfectly dressed and held together however a few hours in, once the games commence, life all of a sudden gets quite interesting for those who took the chance in going commando underneath the garb. Vicars and tarts is another good one for a giggle in that you get to come along as either, depending on how confident you feel.

Hitting the town

In every large town or city there will be *student night,* which is essentially the idea for clubs or pubs to fill their venues with students on an otherwise lacking day of the week, simply because no one else wants to go clubbing on a Tuesday/Wednesday/etc. Entry fees are generally dropped and the prices are once again more reasonable, so long as you can produce your student ID. So that dodgy photo stamped card you had to queue six hours for on day one does have some privileges and benefits attached after all, so don't lose it. Thus you and your mates can head off into town on an otherwise lacklustre night and paint it whatever colour you students feel like, as there will be no one other than students about to complain.

The first port of call for many student groups heading out on the lash (even before the local pub) is likely to be the few tinnies you have before you leave. There are plenty of times I recall hearing of students complaining about the price of going out, so they crack open a few before they go anywhere in that hope that they won't be quite so thirsty when they get to their destination. Thus they feel a reduced need to neck the first few draught beers and are already happily on their way towards a messy kebab flavoured vomit session in the back of a taxi heading home, plus saving a few quid in the process. Of course there is an inherent danger in this tactic in that once this is the established norm the tendency is to get half cut before going out. This is, of course, a slippery slope leading to occasions where I've heard of amazing nights out, where people got so blottoed on a bottle of vodka, before they even left the campus gates, they puked in the taxi on the way there. Of course the night probably was as "amazin'" as they say, but they are equally unlikely to have recalled most of it, half asleep in the corner of the club whilst their friends are busy drawing penises on their comatose face. I think the message here is simple: go out to have a good time and if you happen to have a few too many, well... it happens; don't get trollied in order to go out to have a good time. You don't wipe your bum *before* taking a dump do you?

Now when going out, the first rule of hitting the town is to try and remember that you're no longer in the student bar. The normal rules of dipping your balls into Joe Blog's pint every time he goes to the toilet might not make the bar staff smile as sweetly as those at the campus bar. Also there are chunder rules for the classier venues in town; go puke elsewhere is the general consensus of most pubs and bars; puke inside the establishment and expect to have more chance of being served another pint than a girl guide asking for the yard of ale. No one likes cleaning up someone else's vomit, especially if they are selling you the beer at a discounted rate.

Another important factor to remember when going out on the lash with a bunch of your mates is that the normal time for most other (non-student) people going out tends to differ from the "what's the time? It's beer o'clock" attitude you may get used to with your student colleagues. Therefore it may easily slip your intoxicated mind, as you are breaking in the third verse with "Yogi's knob is long and green, cucum, cucum-bear," that there is a young family at the next table desperately trying to distract their children's attention to learning the lyrics as they wait for their lunch time starters. Also if, or indeed when, this situation does occur, eat humble pie and leave when you're asked to leave. No points are scored for pissing off the locals and you just limit your options for future outings. It's also quite embarrassing to be picked up by the scruff of the neck and tossed out on your arse. It's also more embarrassing to have the police be called out to have a chat with you and letting you sleep it off at the local nick. Furthermore your course leader won't be holding you in high regard if you cause them more work than they cause you.

However treating your locals with respect and getting to know the bar staff can be of value to you. Firstly, you never know when you might need a job, and bar work for students is the nearest you'll get to having a laugh whilst at the same time earning some much needed cash. I know of someone who got to know a local pub, started working there and then moved in with the landlord and lady into their spare room soon afterwards. This secured decent digs at a low cost with people who she became good friends with. She could afford to maintain a decent car and got to eat well in the process. Additionally if you ever want a bolthole away from your digs, popping into your local friendly pub in the day time to order a coffee and have time to read some of your course material might just suit your academic needs nicely.

So when the pubs are exhausted and you and the lads are all beered up and raring to go, it's off to the clubs to perform some magic on the dance floors. I personally hate clubbing and for good reason:

- You have to pay to get in! Even on a student night, when entry is usually reduced, I resent not knowing whether you are walking into a pumping party zone or a club with less life than the local morgue.

- The beer usually tastes like cat's piss. For the record I've never tasted cat's piss however I'm taking an educated guess here.

- It's usually so dark that if you are lucky enough to manage talking to someone you fancy, there is the distinct chance that the following day when the lighting is returned to normal and your beer goggles are removed that you start to regret your advances. Furthermore, and even worse, is when they look at you and you know they are thinking the same.

- The music is so loud you have to become an expert in lip reading or instinctively have the ability to nod in the right places when people are speaking to you.

- Dancing. I've nothing against the skills employed by someone talented enough to look good on the dance floor. What I do have issue with is the fact that I, like many blokes, instinctively lose all of my inhibitions after a certain number of pints and start to really believe that I can boogie down with the best of them. There are vague memories of me being able to clear dance floors quicker than if I was holding a hand grenade in the air whilst shouting "this is it, I'm really going to do it this time." Incidentally that might have been a more dignified ending. I guess I'm not the only one out there who has the rhythmical coordination of a new born foal.

- Watching other people dance. It only encourages the irrational thought of how hard can it really be? I again refer you to the point above.

- The beer usually tastes like sweaty testicles. Again...

- The gorillas on the door are typically only one small step away from needing a pair of jack boots and questioning everyone if their papers are in order. Now I know of a few people who are lovely, well adjusted and kind hearted souls who also work the occasional doors to local clubs. I think it's no coincidence however that almost every other doorman I've ever met seems to have traits of both a paranoid and narcissistic disorder. There are nice ones out there (thank you for reading this and please don't hit me), but the truth is because they have to deal with drunken pillocks on a regular basis, the job turns them into bigger control freak fascists than my wife at Christmas time.

On the plus side there are some positives. The clubs are generally where the girls are, and for a bunch of lads out on the razz, at the end of the night, this is often of significant appeal. Most women are actually relatively coordinated enough not to make dancing look painful; so there's additional benefits to standing around the side of the dance floor, desperately trying to look too cool to strut your stuff. Just pretend to enjoy your pint of feline wizz.

A brief but important warning

In all seriousness, alcohol is something that should be treated with a sensible word of caution. Alcohol dependency is not pretty. It destroys the lives of many people and has a long lasting and severe impact on their families too. In my experience it would be unrealistic to expect students to never overindulge in the many different things on offer at university. Part of being young is making mistakes *but* also learning by them. This is not an endorsement to be stupid and go smoke crack cocaine, however alcohol carries a special penalty for those who drink too much in that it totally ruins prospects, careers, reputations and lives in the long run for those that don't respect it. The danger is that it does it insidiously. I can't imagine there is an alcoholic alive today who thought that they stood a serious chance of ever becoming alcohol dependent; they wouldn't have ever lifted the glass to their lips in the first place. I don't wish to labour the point but take heed that the above content of this chapter should be read in the context of making personal choices to have fun in moderation. This is also not to sound like a blatant government health warning for liability reasons, but more an appeal to common sense please.

Furthermore the short term consequences can also be unpleasant. I know I make light of vomiting in the back of taxis, etc. however when it happens to you it's not going to be pleasant, plus you also stand the chance of being chucked out in the middle of god knows where, at god knows what time of the night/morning. Also if you were fortunate enough to pull, the person you're with is going to very rapidly develop a really important reason as to why they need to be anywhere other than with you.

The other concern of course is that alcohol often makes us disinhibited. This is when we are more likely to carry out behaviours that are out of character for us as a norm. Therefore don't be surprised when you're picked up by the local fuzz and thrown in the nick simply because you thought it was "a good idea at the time" to take a dump in the town centre coin fountain or getting your knob out in the kebab shop. Additionally there are other risks involved other than getting nobbled by the rozzers. There are frequent occasions in every town or city on a Friday night where you will see people inadvertently stumbling out in front of traffic or trying to impress the ladies with a show of chest beating in view of the nearest bouncers. A&E is not the most fun place to be late at night.

In the morning after every night out, the student halls will resound with cries of "never again" and general whimpering noises emanating from bathrooms. Let us not forget that booze is effectively a diluted lethal poison that causes amongst other things significant dehydration. The more you mix it, and the more you binge, the greater the chances of a nasty hangover the next day that may or may not be accompanied with a torrent of vomiting and a not-so-friendly dose of the squits. Hangovers are not nice and trust me, the older you get the worse they are. So make sure that before you go to bed you drink plenty of water. Leave a glass of water and a note for yourself next to your bed as a reminder to rehydrate before you crash and you'll have a better time of it the next day I promise you.

Something else worth considering is simply to space your drinks out a little. There's no harm in having a shandy or soft drink in between your pints. No one need ever know and you'll stand a slightly better chance of not making a total arse of yourself, or at least not before someone else does. You'll also be a little less dehydrated the next morning and your liver will quietly be grateful. The other thing is to resist the compulsion to throw every drink down your neck like it's going out of fashion, thus also saving a few extra quid in the process.

Top tip: After a heavy night out, bed spin is my personal nemesis. If you're one of the lucky ones who never suffers this then good on you for not knowing the torment endured by many of us. Picture being strapped in to a falling aircraft that's lost all control and is whipping round in circles any which way, just waiting to hit the ground. Well, there is a cure. I've found that as soon as the bed spin starts the trick is to simply imagine that you're on a roller coaster. It might not feel overly pleasant, especially when all you need is sleep, however it feels more controlled and the chances of vomit on the curtains is significantly reduced. I've passed this little gem on to quite a few friends who also swear by it.

Now if you find yourself unexpectedly in the position of starting to think that you can't possibly go without a drink then you might be starting to develop a dependency. Alcohol dependency is something that does not suddenly hit you in the face one day. Rather, it creeps up on you like a ninja on special ops, and people find themselves making all sorts of excuses as to why they simply ought to go get drunk. Alcoholics are great at fooling others but they are frequently more devious towards themselves, so if you get to the point, whether at uni or later in life, of recognising a pattern of all too often consumption, then help can be discreetly sought.

There are various sources of information on the internet however an honest and confidential face to face with your GP might just be the ticket. Your choice, but please be honest with yourself.

Illicit Substances

This section is going to be brief and somewhat to the point. The rationale here is to not labour the issue and teach granny to suck eggs. Street drugs are going to be available at uni and there is possibly going to be a point in the next three to four years when you will be given the choice to experiment with whatever is offered to you. That choice might fall in to the category of brief experimentation in your young adult life and may have minimal consequences if you're lucky, or it might just transpire as the turning point when you completely fell off the rails and turned into an utter tit as your life went down the toilet. The problem that most young people face is twofold: firstly, it is everyone's natural presumption that *other* people become drug addicts and secondly, when we're young we have a tendency to feel a tad invincible. This blinkered attitude towards life is not unique and I believe that we all will have or have had points in our lives when we felt like this. I also suspect that it happens more with younger people in their mid to late teens. Few people wake up at 40 years old and think "you know what? I've not dabbled with illicit substances before. Now where can I get a crack pipe at this time in the morning?"

Of course you should also know that when the police nick you for possession of illicit substances, they might not always come across as particularly caring and understanding about your brief experimental phase and the blemish to your otherwise spotless academic record and rise to glory as the benevolent and wonderful human being you will become. Future job applications highlighting disclosed criminal convictions might sit fine in some fast food establishments, but not the classier ones.

Another consideration ought to be that such substances will potentially have the opposite impact on you that you were otherwise hoping. There are plenty of cases where people wind up in a psychiatric hospital experiencing a very unpleasant full blown psychotic episode due to them experimenting with drugs (or legal highs) for the first time. Further to this there is also the risk of serious physical complications. Heart attacks are not cool. Also choking on your own vomit is not going to make dear ol' ma and pa proud. Then there are the long term complications. Lack of money, possible addiction and let's not forget all of the wonderful and charming friends that drug addicts tend to keep.

Your drug dealer is no doubt an otherwise outstanding model citizen who in his spare time does voluntary work down at the local food bank when he's otherwise not working as the lollipop man at the school crossing. Of course the average drug dealer, in an attempt to skim off the top a little will be tempted to mix whatever drug it is you're taking with some mystery ingredient. More mixing equals more profits. And all of the unhealthy benefits get passed directly on to the customer. How would you feel leaving your local take away pizza place to open your food and discover they're saving money on cheese by mixing it with sawdust?

It might seem daft that you'd even consider accepting this scenario, so why would you entertain snorting washing powder, talc or god knows what else your cocaine might be cut with? I don't mean to try and scare anyone here; I'm simply highlighting a fraction of the negative impact that drugs can have on people. There is a trade off between a possible (not guaranteed) high moment in exchange for a plethora of health risks. However if there is only one message worth taking note of, it is this: no matter what anyone says to you, unless you are physically held down and forced to take it, drugs are a matter of your own choices in this life. Peer pressure is not an excuse. Peer pressure wouldn't make you play Russian Roulette with a revolver. People have the ability to make decisions following weighing up the pros and cons when it comes to drug use. A word of advice: choose in advance.

Chapter 7: Money

One of the most memorable pieces of advice about uni that someone ever shared with me was, "it's all about learning to have a good time with no money." Oh how true this is! Arriving at uni, most people have some spare cash in their back pockets. You've just got your student loan, bursary (if you're lucky), or Great Aunt Ethel left you a few extra quid in her will with explicit instruction that you spend this on academic texts and soap. You arrive, as do most others, with a plan for some limited mild fun and frolics and are anticipating being ever so mature and getting down to your course work pretty quickly. There is an internal vision that you have it within you to be the pinnacle example of what a good student should be. You arrive in your halls, empty your life from your suitcase into your room, polish off your best accent or pair of rounded (and don't these make me look studenty and intelligent) glasses and head off to the bar to meet your fellow scholars. All of a sudden and with no less surprise than a priest caught with a loyalty card at a brothel, you discover the magical delights that are on offer at the student bar. Furthermore, to add the cherry to the naughty cake, you buy your first pint and suspect the bar tender serving you must have had a minor mathematical seizure inside their head and accidentally dropped the decimal point in your change to your favour. Student bars are often dirt cheap, and they're run by students who are generally, as far as employees also go, dirt cheap also.

One thing leads to another and before you know it freshers' week has passed in a hazy blur and your IQ is no higher than when you started two weeks ago. The problem that's getting in the way of your planned rise to academic greatness is the simple fact that you have discovered something unexpected: people who are just like you. There are so many new faces arriving at uni that within a few weeks you won't be able to be anything other than drawn to those with similar interests, hobbies, bad habits, etc. as you. Well done, you have a social life... and quite possibly a better one developing than any you ever had before. Of course the problem now is that all of a sudden some nasty tutors have obviously decided that this needs sabotaging by staging inconvenient lectures, seminars, essays, etc. On the flip side you might start to reflect that this should not be such a bad idea due to the fact that Great Aunt

Ethel's inheritance has since disappeared on late night vodka slammer thingies, kebabs and an unplanned taxi seat valet bill.

So you're totally skint, way before you expected to be, and slowly the idea sinks in that *eating* rather surprisingly trumps *partying* on the hierarchy of social needs and requirements for staying alive in modern day society. But do not fear! There are a few life-lines out there that can help you out before the need for a humanitarian aid airdrop is called in.

Please note that this chapter does not seek to explain or teach you how to budget. I don't know whether you've got more money than sense or are considering selling one of your kidneys to cover next week's rent. What is intended here is a general guide or some basic ideas as to how you can manage to get by on relatively little, whilst at the same time not resorting to social isolation or selling yourself to slavery as the only means to make it through uni financially.

Budgets and bugger its

There are some great books out there about budgeting. I'm guessing you've never felt the urge to read one before but you're feeling that urge well up inside you right now, aren't you? Are you not starting to realise that complicated and highly planned budgeting practices are essential skills that might just get you through the next few years before resorting to prostituting yourself at the local docks. No?!!?? Me neither.

When I started uni for my first degree I knew I was skint, and what money I had, I had to spread out a bit. However I did feel like I was going to make it through the first term financially and the only budgeting methods I employed were simple: don't buy what you don't need, don't buy expensive shit and become a little more humble in your standards. Budgeting *skills* were something for managing my money when I actually had more to manage than I had in my pocket; for when I had kids, a mortgage, etc. The trouble is that uni life gets in the way. That £20 you had to get you through the weekend somehow seems trivial when your mates are all off to the uni bar for happy hour and this is your ticket to a cracking good laugh with the boys. Suddenly, come Saturday morning, there is the *bugger it* moment and the realisation that you're going to have to find some economy throw together pasta meals for the equivalent of the 19p you have left in your jeans.

Some financial concerns you can't avoid

- Your student fees. You don't have to be studying astrophysics to have the wherewithal to realise that the uni won't take kindly to you prioritising pimping up your crib over paying the tuition fees. Uni is an expensive business for you and it literally is a business for them, so they won't let you do it on a tab. Course fees unfortunately do needing paying.

- Rent. Unless you live in your car or a box in the subway, you will be obliged to pay some sort of rent, so let's be sensible about this one. Our huge overdraft facility and student loan might briefly make us feel like millionaires, but staying in the penthouse suite of the Ritz will eat through the cash flow faster than the spread of nits at a hippy convention. Whilst student halls are frequently more crowded than a hurricane refugee centre they are relatively cheap(ish), they are usually clean(ish) and they are also bloody good fun. Living out in a big shared house is also not to be overlooked. Whilst there are sometimes issues with personal privacy and a few other things already mentioned in a previous chapter, if shared with enough people they can help divide some of the respective costs of not dying of malnutrition or hypothermia.

- Debt. Well if you can avoid this one, the chances are you have daddy's credit card, are expecting to inherit the family business and let's hope the title is also hereditary. For the rest of the real world, incurring some debt as a student is a necessary evil. There are, however, bad and then worse ways of getting into debt. On the *not so great* side of the scale we might think about student loans, bank overdraft, etc. On the *positively evil and selling your soul* side are the credit cards, store cards, etc. You may as well call out "Beelzebub" three times in mirror backwards at midnight whilst sacrificing a chicken as a quicker alternative to signing up for a preferential rate credit card. There are benefits to minimising the amount of debt you incur so try to remember this when you are given your extra grand or two, and also recognise the pit falls in acting like this week's lottery winner.

- The bank.

A clever young man from Sri Lanka
Aspired to be a rich banker.
He gave everyone loans
Then took away their homes.
On his bonus it said "what a wanker."

Whilst each bank will claim to be acting in the best interests of students, they are also a necessary evil. Their smiling promises of "here have a student overdraft at a reduced rate" (or even for free) is not in fact free cash. At the end of the day please remember that banks are not charitable organisations and they are not there to simply look after your cash for you because your pockets are simply not big enough. They are in fact playing the long game. Your overdraft won't likely be free forever and what they are primarily interested in, is not what they can do for you whilst you're a student; they will however quite like you to feel obliged to remain with them and in debt to them after your degree is complete. By this time you will likely have more debt than Uganda and you know what? Your student friendly bank will happily give you a happy loan to go with the big happy smiles. This will come with a structured repayment plan and huge amount of interest. But make sure you have a job or you've got no chance. I had a bank ask me if I'd like a loan after I completed my degree to cover my overdraft facility I had with them (which was still at an agreed student rate for a period of time). What they were asking me in effect was whether I'd like to consolidate something that only gave them minimal interest payments for something which I'd be paying through the nose for. Image going into the doctors with the sniffles and being asked if you've like a nice dose of the clap to take your mind off it.

> **Top tip: Beware anyone suggesting you come collect your free money. You might find that you're required to grit your teeth and bend over quite far to pick it up.**

- Taxes. You may be a poor student but you still have to pay some of your respective taxes, whether they be road tax on your vehicle or national insurance on your bar job pay packet. Just because you're an emaciated student doesn't mean you will be entitled to a completely free ride. Things can be a lot cheaper for you, especially if you're quite savvy about your cash flow, however there will still be certain responsibilities you are legally required to meet otherwise the academic period of your life might finish a lot quicker than planned.

Some things you might not want to avoid

- Insurance. Who needs insurance? Companies

selling policies by frightening people to take out cover for events that are never going to happen. When I first went to study at uni the most expensive thing in my room was a knackered old TV that may as well have been filled with house bricks for all it weighed and the dodgy signal reception. If you stood far enough away you could, sort of, make out the picture. There was also the problem that if the dynamics of the room changed suddenly (such as someone else rudely and unexpectedly walking in) it would have a minor tantrum and refuse to work unless someone caressed the aerial whilst also hanging out of the window. If someone had nicked it they would have done me a favour. Getting insurance cover in this instance might have been a bit of overkill, however consider what *you* might be taking to uni. I'll hazard a guess that your smart-phone might be worth a few hundred quid to buy new. Laptop? TV? A few quid on a small contents insurance policy probably won't be a bad idea when you consider the cost of replacing your stuff. Alternatively your accommodation and door to your room might rival the security arrangement of Fort Knox, in which case no worries. However I recall the first room I had at uni. There was an old fashioned lock on the door that you could have picked with a paperclip and a light breeze. In fact one day my roommate and I found our whole room stolen. Fortunately it was just for a prank but things really do go missing from time to time. Whilst you're not intentionally going to give the local tea leaf an easy time of it, why take the chance?

- The student loan. I know I've already mentioned that tactical avoidance of as much debt as possible is a desirable objective, but for many avoidance of all debt isn't a realistic option. Student loans serve as cheaper ways of getting your hands on some much needed cash. Just avoid the temptation to think *I could really manage a new Playstation right now,* unless you've really budgeted with some vague attempt at considering what you will need to live on and not die before the end of term. Student loans don't have to be paid until you're in big pants and working with a grown up's salary however they are not bottomless pits of wonga.

- Spare change. Seriously? Yes. Get an old tin and stick your loose change in it whenever you can. Promise yourself that you won't raid it and don't even count it until something dire happens and you need some money in a hurry that you otherwise wouldn't have. You might need an unexpected coach ticket home for some reason and you'll be glad of it when you would otherwise be up the creak. A word of caution borne from experience: big, chunky, fat cigars for the Summer Ball unfortunately shouldn't count as an emergency.

- Paying the bill. Not the Old Bill necessarily but rather settling your accounts ASAP. If you bought something on credit, get it settled as soon as you are able before whatever company starts to think that sending you late payment charges must be what you really want, seeing as you must have so much spare cash. Alternatively if you can't pay something back immediately, a friendly call to whatever company, to politely explain that you ought to prioritise eating this month might be helpful. In my experience speaking to such companies won't earn their warm affections, however they usually prefer it if you pay off your debt in smaller chunks before you go into hiding and file off your fingerprints. Better still is not getting into this sort of debt in the first place.

- Hardship funds. There are usually some hardship funds available that can be attained via the university's administration team. You'll have to do some digging at your particular uni however the general premise for these funds is that in times of hardship, when all else fails, you can seek some assistance with the uni to see if they can help financially somewhat. Now don't get me wrong in that this is not a *free beer, get it here* fund. This is for students who would otherwise need to quit the course because they simply cannot afford it. It's a lifeline for those desperate enough to ask, and make no mistake in that you'll be asked to jump through numerous hoops, including opening your financial details for them to scrutinise before they give you anything. They are obviously open to being scammed and as such they might lose funds that desperately needy students, later down the line, may not otherwise get. So don't be a prick and go asking for hardship funding unless you *really* need it. And if you really need it don't be afraid to ask.

- Student discounts. Keep your ID card on you and don't forget to flash to save cash. Cheap cinema tickets, cheap travel cards, etc. Just remember that buying loads of cheap discounted stuff that you don't need is a saving only in your imagination, no matter how hard the impulsive part of your brain might try and tell you otherwise.

- Making the call home. I've included this here but this should not be viewed as an automatic fund. If your parents are loaded and they choose to throw stupid amounts of money at you, well

that's their own issue and your short term gain.
You'll learn nothing about coping when the
cash flow runs dry at some point in your later
life, but realistically who's going to offer to
struggle when they have a money tree. The
majority though will likely come to a point
where they have to ask the old dears for a few
extra quid in order to keep their heads above
water (or in beer). So don't be afraid to ask
when necessary, but like most parents, whilst
there is usually a willingness to help out dear
Johnny when he needs new text books, the
supply is likely to dry up pretty fast when he's
requesting enough money to fit out a library. So
use this option lightly and only when you really
have to. The main point here is about well
planned timing and common sense. To set the
scenario, Johnny eventually builds up the
courage to call home to ask his folks for a few
hundred extra notes. The first problem is of the
Dutch courage variety; try not calling them at
3AM on a week day after you've been out all
night and are totally tanked up. When dad picks
up the phone there's going to be two potential
thoughts going through his mind: "Aunt Ethel's
finally croaked" or "if that's my pissed up git of
a son calling in the middle of the night again
because he desperately needs more vodka
thingies, I'm going to cut his balls off". Either

way, a speedy cheque in the post might not be finding its way to your door.

- Public transport. Whilst taxi rides back to their respective residence is a no-nonsense method of travel for many a businessman, for the average student, unless you feel you can outrun them without paying the bill and avoid getting run over in the process, then public transport might be the more economically sound method of travel. Now the thing about public transport is that it's not only a far cheaper way to travel but environmentally friendly for the eco warriors among you. You might also be able to get some really good deals if you flash your student ID at the right time. There are some considerations though:

  o The waiting. Oh my god, how many precious hours of my life have I lost waiting for buses? Usually when it's totally tipping it down too. Also there has been more than one occasion when the bus driver simply drove past or I was distracted and didn't flag it down in time. If all that extra time could somehow be put into something productive I could probably have studied for an extra degree.

  o The shame. I really have heard people moan

about the stigma of using public transport before. Okay, usually they're acting like a hormonal 13 year old but come on! I have honestly heard the words "but buses are gay" before. As far as I am aware this country's public transportation methods do not relate to sexual preferences. If you're a regular student without HRH in front of your name then there's no shame in slumming it and riding the bus.

o   The other occupants. Admittedly there might some particularly odorous, dishevelled, unsightly and in all likelihood pissed up individuals that use the buses from time to time. But let's put you and your friends aside for one moment. You're going to get quite a few disapproving stares if you act like a complete tosser, spilling your kebab all over the place as you try to find your mouth whilst the bus bounces about on its journey. There's always one weirdo on the bus. Don't let it be you.

- Get a bike. Unleash the modern day hippy hipster in you and get a cheap bike to run you about town. You don't have to be a season ticket holder for Greenpeace rallies to warrant getting a cheap set of wheels. Basic maintenance is generally fairly straight forward and won't cost the Earth. Also you'll be saving squirrels in their thousands and your legs will be looking beefcake in no time. Just watch out for bus drivers mowing you down as they're distracted by students vomiting kebab over their other passengers.

- Internet bargains. Sites such as Ebay are wonderful ways of recycling old books that would otherwise become door stops, or picking up cheap deals that would cost a mint elsewhere.

- The library. Remember that having your very own book that you're going to read five pages out of and costing you £40 is easily avoidable when you have the library. That's £40 more pasta to see you through the next three years.

Some things you definitely want to avoid

- Tea leafs. Please don't associate yourself with those individuals who opt for the five fingered discount as the preferable method of obtaining their goods. Even if you're behaving yourself, if you get caught in a shop with a wally of a friend, who is rumbled whilst discreetly trying to pocket a three piece suite, you may also be had by association. Shop owners don't give a crap about your supposed innocence when they're trying to set an example to other would be cat burglars. So unless you can make an exit like a super villain, don't do it. Furthermore, those that see shops as easy targets might also be the same type to help themselves to your pasta rations and more.

- Selling illegal stuff. Whether it's stolen goods, drugs or Calvin Klein genuine article *honest guvnor* handbags, there's no quicker way to get a dodgy reputation and a visit from the old bill, because people talk.

- Get rich quick schemes. For a small investment you have the opportunity to make lots of friends and also be on your way to making your first million. What could possibly go wrong? The unfortunate truth is that if these schemes really worked everyone would be doing it. And herein lies the problem: you will be given the impression that the only mugs are the ones at the bottom of the pyramid. But don't worry, you just have to encourage and train them to sell the product and before you know it they'll be just a rich as you. They only need to buy the stock through you and you'll be making cash whilst you sleep. Pyramid sales have a bad reputation for being a crafty way of working on poor people's vulnerabilities in them trying to find easier ways of earning a living. It also seeks to get those same people doing the dirty work for the company by having a free sales force. Imagine you're the company boss who puts down his fat, juicy cigar for a moment and has a great idea. Instead of paying out large amounts of cash on advertising and sales, you employ clever and manipulative people to not only sell your product to the public, but also persuade those customers to become free sales people. There are many people who have ended up with rooms in their homes filled with worthless crap, believing they are their own boss or some sort of company executive. Pyramid sales are no longer called pyramid sales (due to their dodgy reputation) but the basic principles are the same. Fat cats will get the cream, their executive staff get a big slice, but the cut lessens and the work increases the more down the line. By the time it reaches you, you're not the company boss man that you're being told you will be and the cream and cake has already been digested several times over.

- Payment by commission jobs. The reason that these jobs pay by commission is that in 9 times out of 10 they can pay you far less for the same amount of effort and hours worked. Seriously, avoid these with a much enthusiasm as you would dodge a boot in the nadgers.

- Work that will pay you "just as soon as the contract's finished. Honest". You're a student, not an illegal immigrant builder. Don't waste your time.

- Laziness. Or is it poor motivation? Whatever you want to call it, getting off your arse and finding some part time work will help break up the partying, studying or both. It will earn you some means to be a little more self sufficient and you can hold your head high in the knowledge that you made a positive difference to the quality of your life all by yourself.

Some more general guidance about jobs

I've held down a few part time jobs in my time as a student. It's not all about demeaning yourself by dressing like a giant chicken and holding a discount store sign in the middle of town. There are some reasonable and even some great jobs out there that will help top up the living fund, so it's worth being pragmatic and proactive in your approach to bagging one.

The worst and at the same time possibly one of the best jobs I had as a student was working for the university campus housekeeping team. This was a holiday job, so when the halls were emptied at the end of term, a bunch of us stayed back as the uni rented out accommodation to foreign students and conferences. Whilst unblocking the toilet where King Kong took his daily dump is not the best of memories, there was also the total giggle we had when left to our own devices to get on with our work. I've also worked in the canteen pot wash for a while. Not fun. The kitchen dictatorship starts with the head chef and goes all the way down to the pot wash weasels at the bottom of the pile. Half way through the shift we'd get a free meal. It's funny how everyone else felt the urge to sit on a different table to the smelly pot wash boys. At the other end of the scale I got to work several nights a week in the campus bar, which felt like being paid to be social with my mates, and also have the odd beer of course. It was a great laugh and a must have part time job if you can land this one. Some of the best things about working in the student bar:

- Everyone knows who you are.

- You get paid for hanging about in the prime social area of campus.

- Everyone is your friend, especially when they want to get served first.

- There are numerous comedy moments to be had. Pissed up students trying to impress other pissed up students is a recipe for both disaster and hilarity.

- Free beer. Not the Stolen Artois type. Kind people will often put one behind the bar for you.

- Easy hours that often fit outside of lecture times.

- Did I mention the free beer?

At the end of the day having a part time job will be a bit of a drag at times. There will be occasions when the last thing you need is to be hauling yourself out of bed to go work for a pittance. The alternative is not having any additional cash flow and in my experience a little part time work is a good thing to get used to. You will more likely appreciate the money you have and furthermore, parents and hardship fund charities are more likely to help out when you're in need if they can see you also making an effort to be self sufficient. You'll have a little more pride and you will also make quite a few extra friends along the way. And let's not forget that when you finally graduate you can sit opposite your potential new employer in your first interview and send them a clear message that you're not some work-shy slacker by the fact that you held down a part time job throughout your studentship. Employers respect those that demonstrate keenness with hard work more that those that demonstrate it with their collection of beer bottles and the ability to blag money from granny.

Simple pitfalls and some final don'ts. Don't:

- ...lend other people cash. You might as well ask the local fox to guard your prize winning chicken as expect a speedy return on lending other students cash. Lending friends money when you have some and they don't might give you a good, lovely, heart-warming feeling. A week later when they are due to pay you back (because that's when you said you'd need it by as you have to buy your Summer Ball ticket), and your new best mate in the whole wide world is nowhere to be seen, then you're likely to get a little hacked off. The advice here is to be extra careful in ever lending anyone money. In my experience this is a good life long lesson, not just whilst you're a student. On the other hand you don't need to turn into some self absorbed Scrooge with no friends. The very simple solution here is that if someone asks you to lend them money, assume you will never get it back from them. That way you won't give any essential reserves away with any expectations attached. You won't alienate otherwise great friends that might start avoiding you simply because they're bad with cash and owe you a fiver. Giving a friend money to help them out is a much more friendly thing to do, and because you're not holding them over a barrel you don't have to turn into the local mafia representative to get it back. A simply "pay me back when you afford to" means you keep your friends, you protect yourself from impulsive generosity and of course they will never ask you again unless they have paid you back what you already gifted.

- ...borrow money from other students. For all of the reasons above. If you borrow and then for whatever reason can't afford to pay it back (when you swore on Great Auntie Brunhilda's grave you'd have it by Tuesday), you might feel the need to make like a mole and go to ground. It's better to miss out on some things by not having the cash than missing out on friends when you can't return their generosity. Good mates are far more valuable than money.

- ...think your part-time job has your name etched into it. Just because you get on with your boss there is no reason to let them down by pretending to be ill so you can skip a shift to attend the house party you just heard about. News travels and there is always someone ready to take your job if you get ratted out. Also your reliability record speaks for itself. If you need unexpected time off, simply ask. Okay it makes sense to offer something else to appease the situation, e.g. agreeing to work a few extra shifts or whatever, so there might be some trade-off. Honesty with your employer, even when they say no to your request, earns you brownie points that do stack up. The employer/employee relationship is a two way deal and in my working career I've found that most employees will give extra consideration to those who show willingness and honesty.

- ...assume that everyone else has loads of cash. Most people don't. It just feels like everyone else having a good time out on the tiles has more than a tenner in their pocket. If you're in the company of other students on a night out, the chances are that there's enough in spare change coppers in pockets to manufacture a transatlantic underwater cable. Just because people are keen to go out doesn't mean they're loaded and like you they may well be scraping the financial barrel.

- ...hide away in your room. Remember, it's all about learning to have a good time with no money.

Chapter 8: Relationships and Sex

When you're at school in the middle of the early to mid-teen, hormonal, spot infested, can't sit on a bus without getting a motion induced raging erection phase, relationships can often be a bit of a learning curve. In other words you were probably a little bit crap at it. Remember the line about "my friend asked me to ask you to ask your friend if they think that my friend's alright". Sound familiar? Not a particularly effective method for igniting the relationship that blows Romeo and Juliet off the top spot, but this is frequently an important hurdle for most youngsters learning about how personal relationships are formed. By the time we reach uni we are more likely to be at the more mature stage of dropping the middleman and are able to recognise the subtle nuances of flirting with intent. There's that and there's also the alcohol fuelled, late night, "wanna bump uglies?" approach, but either way the chances are that emotional and sexual relationships are probably going to have their place in your life during your three years at uni. And for many these years will be a continuation of (but not a complete maturing of) the "my friend fancies yours" business that started years before.

For some the most traumatic part of going to uni is that they will have to leave their life-long love (of 3.5 weeks) back at home, or even worse, with them going to uni elsewhere in the country. They part with enthusiastic promises of writing/emailing/phoning/sexting every five minutes, then with a parting tear, a tender kiss and quick fondle in the bus station, they leave with promises of not even talking to anyone else of the opposite sex and declarations of how desperately lonely their existence will now be. Fast forward to mid way freshers' week and numerous pints down the line, all of a sudden other people start to look quite attractive. What's her face back at home won't worry about what she doesn't know about, and before you know it you convince yourself that you're only being pleasant and polite towards the friendly lass you're dribbling over who you've already mentally nick-named *Thunder-Jugs*.

I can think of very few people who had an ongoing relationship back home that survived the duration of the degree. No doubt there are some and good luck to them, but like hide and seek champs, they don't come out very often. On the other hand there are quite a few romances that start at uni and blossom in to long term relationships. That's not to say that there's not a lot of flash in the pan relationships, but the point I'm trying to make is that when you're going to spend more of your life at uni rather than home, those relationships that stand the test of time also seem to be the ones where people see each other with the greatest frequency.

Sex

Most relationships start off on the premise of *I like you* and *you like me,* which are the typical building blocks for any friendship. Whereas *I like you* with a subtle hint of *can I have a gander at what's in your pants?* is really what most adult personal relationships lead to pretty quickly. Sex at uni is one of those things that, for many people, is still relatively new territory. Of course freshers' is not exclusively full of soon to be ex-virgins. There are many that have broken the seal on this one well before uni, but the difference is that in your halls of residence you don't have to hide away from your mum and dad. You can bonk like rabbits on amphetamines as much as you like and it might just feel like you've discovered something new, naughty and grown up all at the same time. It can sort of be like the alcohol thing: a feeling of "because I'm allowed to do this I'm going to try and take it to a whole new level". And for some strange reason alcohol is often involved, at least to some extent. Booze sometimes loosens both inhibitions and bra straps.

There is a very liberating feeling to attending university and no longer living under your parent's wings. Sex can very quickly seem like it is the focal point of your studies. Discovering new and wonderful methods and places in which to develop your skills in this field may easily take over much of your existence for a time. Whilst this can be a healthy and fun learning curve in your young adult life just remember that you are not in fact the first to discover it and secondly you don't have to rub it in the face of others who might not be having such a rampant time as you. Then again maybe you're someone who will take a little time before you find the right one you choose to share your bed with. Or maybe you're a total luckless munter. Either way, most people eventually end up in the sack with someone, thus there are some obvious precautions to be considered.

Sexually Transmitted Diseases

Uni halls can sometimes feel a bit like a Roman orgy with enough grinding action to provide the equivalent energy expenditure of a supernova. Thus there are the risks associated with lots of people playing hide the sausage, such as sexually transmitted diseases; many of which are not overly obvious. There also might be times when you get lucky only to go down to discover what appears to be the genital discharge of Swamp Thing. However many STD's are not always so blatant. It might take a little time before you start to suspect that you've contracted knob rot. Alternatively there are STD's where people are carriers but show few or no symptoms. The easiest means in which to avoid getting a dose of the nasty is to either not have sex with anyone or alternatively use a dunky. Condoms are a simple and mostly effective means to not catching the genital lurgy. As an added bonus they can help with you not coming down with an unexpected dose of fatherhood. They are also relatively easy to get your hands on at all hours. Besides, why take any chances? So keep a topped up supply of rubber readies in your room. You don't exactly have to leave them out on display in a punch bowl, but knowing there is a stash of three in your pants draw, that are still reasonably in date, won't go amiss.

Not to go into too much detail about STD's here, but in all seriousness, whilst most can be treated there are some really nasty diseases you can inadvertently contract from people who don't even realise they are a carrier. There is a wealth of resource on the internet and also at your local surgery. So if you happen to have forgotten to suit up the old fella and suspect that you might have caught something icky, the sooner you get down to your GP, the better the prognosis. Also be sensible and don't go jumping in the sack with anyone else until you get the all clear.

Experimentation

There is nothing wrong with safe experimentation with sex when at uni. Young adults are, after all, young. Experimentation means different things for different people though. For many this simply means going at it like a boss with a copy of the karma sutra. For others, finding themselves in a ménage a trios or in quite interesting situations involving a bunch of semi-naked people, a pack of cards or a spinning bottle is not unheard of. Also there are those who will find themselves coming out of the closet and exploring their sexuality. There will also be some who will want to save their virginity for the person who they are going to end up marrying and it is either a religious or moral choice. So whatever choices you make, please remember not to be judgemental or mocking of others. Sexual growth and maturity are just as important as intellectual growth for the relatively balanced and well adjusted young adult you will hopefully be at the end of your time at uni. However, just because people are legally considered adults at 18 years does not make them mature, just as maturity does not make someone wise. Uni is a time of learning and growth, thus allowances should be made for mistakes and cock-ups (pun intended). Be forgiving of yourself and others too.

Common sense

- Don't bang the academic staff. They could get in serious trouble. You will have your performance (academic) questioned.

- Relationships are a period of growth and personal learning. Just because you feel that the person you're currently seeing might just be the perfect one for you, don't expect to get it right all the time. More importantly don't expect them to get it right too. A relationship is much about acceptance of your partner's faults as it is the good stuff. When you first meet someone, no matter how perfect they seem, just like you they can't wait to have a sneaky parp as soon as you leave the room.

- Relationship maintenance is something you will have to get the hang of. People in relationships periodically fall out. If it happens all of the time, then they're probably not the one for you, but the occasional argument is the norm. Make up sex is fun too. Probably not the best reason to fall out though. Telling her she looks like a moose just so you get to have make-up sex is not going to work out too well in the long run.

- Breaking up with someone is sometimes a necessary evil. If things aren't working, grow a pair and finish it with them, face to face. Don't simply cause them anguish for weeks on end by refusing to answer their calls/texts or making blatant excuses. Worst of all would be to be seen rolling in the hay with someone else when you originally told your partner you couldn't go out as you had an important essay to complete.

> *Top tip: Bunches of flowers sometimes go a long way if you do it right, i.e. florists, paying for them, etc. From personal experience I can tell you that impulsive, alcohol fuelled gifts of flowers stolen from a lecturer's garden, are not always received with the enthusiasm in which they were intended. Unfortunately what I actually left soaking in her favourite tea mug was in fact a bunch of spiders. The romantic fool am I?*

Chapter 9: Onwards and upwards

The next three or four years are going to be wonderful. If you're already in uni and reading this then you'll hopefully see there's value in some of these pages that amounts to more than emergency kindling material. And if you're just starting out on your journey you should take comfort in the fact that it's actually quite hard to screw up completely. Yes there are pitfalls and there will be times when you'll mess things up, no matter what you do, but that's part of life. If you can accept this and learn to embrace the fact that there will be periodic screw ups, you'll be more likely to pick yourself up a little better when they happen. I hope that you'll also take with you some small gems of knowledge or advice that will serve you a little better at uni than might otherwise have been the case had you not browsed these pages.

The following few years are, in theory, going to be about learning, yet your books and course material are only one element of this. Remember that the academic side ought to be the focal point of your experience, yet not exclusive of all else. And this is also reflected in the real world at the other end of the higher learning digestive tract. Your future career, whilst important, should not be your sole purpose in life. Work overlaps with family, which overlaps with friendships, which overlaps with health, and so on. University is no different. So live, experience, learn, grow, screw up, and really importantly: try to have some fun while you're doing it. For many people uni is the best three years of their lives. It doesn't have to be however, and there is no point trying to force it, but then again I suspect you might just love your new adventure.

There will also be those that it is not suited to. Some of the friends you will make in the first few weeks will drop out in the period of the first term, but in my experience this is not because uni is not for them, rather they are not ready for uni. There are others who will be catapulted from the battlements for too much larking around or not attending to their studies. The uni staff expect there to be some tomfoolery however they won't officially endorse it. Some people will try again and others will go their own way, but don't let this affect your plans. Your friends will change over the next few years. The people you meet on day one might not necessarily end up being the life-long buddies you hang out with in your final year, but this doesn't really matter. Treat everyone with equal respect and in a manner in which you would want to be treated. People will surprise you and you will surprise yourself too.

Each new academic year will see a growth in your confidence too. Before you know it you'll be feeling all superior and lording it over the new batch of freshers quivering in their boots as they arrive in their droves. So be kind. Remember how anxiety provoking it was trying to find your way around a huge place with a bunch of people you only just met. Have fun with them and be kind. Don't go so far to as to share the secret location of the throne of solitude that only you and that disgruntled cleaning lady know about, but do look out for the noobs. There are people that will be looking out for you on day one (whether you realise it or not). So when you see a fresher looking like a five year old lost in the supermarket isles as they try and find their first class, resist the temptation to send them off looking for the *Mary Huff lecture theatre* and consider actually showing them the way.

Prepare for each new year with enthusiasm and courage, as with each new academic year brings new challenges, both socially and in your studies. And in your final year, which will come all too soon, you will possibly start looking for jobs in your chosen field (or maybe not) and the adventure will begin afresh. Hopefully your mates won't have shaved your eyebrows off in the last six months and you might even start attending interviews. Alternatively you might want to look into doing a bit of travelling after uni. The number of people that have the confidence after uni to simply book a plane ticket and fly off to some remote part of the planet, armed with only a back pack and their sense of humour is amazing. People gradually build the confidence to do things that they wouldn't have thought they could at 18 and so will you.

If the first term is yet to start then expect to be a little apprehensive about all that's ahead. You and every single person who is starting with you are feeling exactly the same right now. The uni staff know this and so do the other students that are now in the second and third years. Be reassured in that there will be loads of people wanting to help in such as manner as they were once helped themselves. Going to uni is one of the best choices that you ever made, I promise you.

Finally, remember that your experiences are more valuable than what money can buy. Make more friends than just your roommate. Try new things and share your experiences with the friends you are yet to make. Learn not just from the lectures and books but also from the stories your friends have to tell. Absorb everything and be like a magpie. Pick through the gems of knowledge that you gleam from others and make them part of you; and don't be afraid to discard the crap. Before you know it you'll be graduating in a silly hat and having a photo taken with your mum whilst trying to hide the shape of that new nipple piercing poking through your shirt.

The big blue yonder

This may seem a little premature right now, especially if you haven't even flown the nest for the university halls as yet, but there is no harm in thinking ahead a little into the realms of what may lie beyond your graduation. Believe me when I say that there is sense in taking a little time for making life goals/ambitions. Some forward planning makes for more positive and structured present day activities. Those that are most successful in this life (and yes this is more loaded than public transport in Cairo) are those that actually make life goals. Therefore going to uni with some idea as to what's going to come afterwards is what the smart kids do.

By the time you get to your final year you should be thinking of doing some prep work. This doesn't have to be overly detailed and meticulously planned to the extent of thinking about a future mortgage, what you're going to call your kids and booking your own plot on the sunny side of St Ethel's. On the other hand having a vague idea of what line of work you're going to be looking to get into would be a start. Where you might want to live (or more importantly where you wouldn't) are also important considerations.

At some point towards the end of your degree it might also be advisable to get to work on a draft of your curriculum vitae. An attractive and polished CV is not something that is handed to you in a moment of divine angelic intervention. Nor will it be delivered to you as an epiphany moment whilst having a jobbie. CV's are *always* work in progress. They start with you getting an idea of the current format of the day (or whatever's presently trendy) and then you fill in the blanks with your personal info. You should try and do it properly the first time, and by this I mean input all of your exam results and dates correctly. Then each and every time you move in your career you update it and move on. So keep it safe. Emailing it to a relative to keep a copy for you might just save you a headache when your hard drive commits suicide the day before the big interview.

> *Top tip: When writing your CV remember you were never an astronaut. The faintest smell of bullshit on a CV won't get you the interview.*

Job interview do's and don'ts:

- Don't get pissed the night before.

- Don't apply for jobs that have only a good pay packet as the only redeeming quality. Cash flow is relative, i.e. most people soon get used to what they're earning and will spend to their means. It's better to earn modestly and enjoy your work than having a great holiday each year to make up for the other 50 weeks of sheer misery or boredom. Work to live, not the other way around.

- Do shave, shower and any of the other S's before the interview.

- Make appropriate eye contact. Eyes cast downward smacks of boredom, confidence issues or you speaking horseshit.

- Sit comfortably rather than stiffly. You'll seem more confident this way. But don't go so far to put your feet up on the furniture or scratch your nut sack. There's also a balance between confidence and being a self adsorbed arse.

- Get there 15 minutes before the interview. Not

half a day before (you'll appear desperate) or just scraping in by the skin of your teeth.

- Ask some questions at the end. Don't try and impress them with questions that you could have easily found out about before hand or using big words you don't really understand. Rather ask some things that make you look like you're really interested not only in what you're applying for but also where, e.g. "is there a social side to the team?", "will you honour existing holiday plans I have?", "are there opportunities for future promotion?" Questions such as "what's the salary?" and "so what do you do here anyway?" will make you look like a plonker.

- Breathe. Not doing so carries somewhat significant consequences.

I could easily write a whole chapter on this however the purpose here is to get you to onside by thinking ahead of the game at little. Whilst this is stuff for the future, forward thinking will help you retain some focus on the purpose of what you do in the present. The university experience can be a little overwhelming at first but it's also possible to get comfortable in the feeling that you're going to be there forever. Three years or more is a long time after all, so why make all the effort in the first or second years? There's plenty of time to pull it all together in the final year isn't there?

Well no there isn't actually. If you don't want to get caught with your trousers down (metaphorically speaking – there will be plenty of other times over the next few years when this probably won't be a metaphor) then having some realisation that each year really does count towards the bigger picture will really help you.

By the time you get to your final year you might also want to consider some basic aspects of acting like a grown up. Not completely however; there will still be time to have some fun, but getting into the habit of drinking/partying slightly less frequently, buying an iron, getting your hair cut more than once a year, shaving with some regularity, and generally starting to get yourself more organised would be wise. As you leave uni you will start to have more and more responsibilities. These don't need to feel like a horror story, but don't take care of the basics and they'll soon turn into one. Traffic cones and yards of ale are going to have to take a back seat to paying your rent and remembering to feed the hamster. Getting into some vague routine doesn't mean you have to start wearing a tie and remembering not to scratch your arse in public, but throttling back, after the escapades of the first few years, will make life a little more manageable when uni comes to an end.

Remember the whole point of uni (for most) is to further your education in order that you can then go out into the workplace with a great job. Some people however will go on to do their Masters and others are there to learn for learning's sake, but for most the experience is a means to a career related end. Working for a living, paying the rent or buying your first washing machine are all going to be part of your life after uni. When you graduate make sure that you leave with valuable memories and experiences. Take with you the contact details of all the people you still want in your life and leave behind those that you don't. Know that uni life is about growing, just as is leaving at the end of it. Life is not so much going to change as develop into something bigger. University may be the best time of your life but it's not the only time, so use it for what it is: learn, live and grow. Use every minute. Plan for the future, but even more importantly, live in the present. Bon voyage!

ABOUT THE AUTHOR

K. Daniel has graduated university twice and has successfully neither been kicked off nor discredited from either course. As a bonus he did learn how not to starve to death in the process. He first attended and attained a semi-respectable Desmond class degree from Oxford University. He studied Theology because he couldn't think of anything else to do with his time, enjoyed uni life a little too much and is still anticipating being struck by lightning. He later found an urge to return to the academic arena, this time as a mature student to study a more vocational degree with Bournemouth University. This time he actually did some work, thus earning him a first class honours degree to match the first class student loan. He presently lives in the South West of England where he has two dogs, two children and a lovely wife who still hasn't got round to divorcing/murdering/burying him yet.